Tapestry

Faith & Forgiveness

Adrian Rogers

Tapestry: Faith & Forgiveness

© 2013 by Love Worth Finding Ministries, Inc.
2941 Kate Bond Road • Memphis, Tennessee 38133

Scripture taken from the New King James Version © 1982 by Thomas Nelson, Inc. Used by permission. All rights reserved.

Excerpts and quotations from *Tapestry: Faith & Forgiveness* may be used in magazines, articles, newsletters, bulletins, and reviews without the written permission of Love Worth Finding Ministries. Each such use must be accompanied by the following credit line:

From *Tapestry: Faith & Forgiveness* © 2013 by Love Worth Finding Ministries. Used by permission.

Any other use of materials in *Tapestry: Faith & Forgiveness*, including the use of complete articles or other content in its entirety must be upon written permission from:

Love Worth Finding Ministries
P.O. Box 38300 • Memphis, TN 38183

Design by Eternity Communications.
Printed in China.

13-digit ISBN: 978-0-9859406-0-7

We gratefully acknowledge the help of the following people in the creation of *Tapestry: Faith & Forgiveness*:

Sheri Ross Saldana, General Editor
Cathy Allen, Contributing Editor
Brandi Hayes, Contributing Editor
Carol Anne Posey, Contributing Editor

If there was ever a time
for an earth-shaking, mountain-moving,
devil-defying, sin-destroying, revival-bringing
faith,
this is the time, this is the age, this is the hour.
And not only do we need to **possess a faith**...
we need to have **a faith
that possesses us**.

—Adrian Rogers

Why "Tapestry"?

"The Bible is like a garment. You pull a thread here, and it wrinkles way over there. It's all tied together."

—Adrian Rogers

The inspiration for *Tapestry* came in part from Dr. Rogers' own words about the unity of the Bible. Add to that what he taught about the Bible being the infallible, inspired, life-giving, life-changing Word of God. What you have is a focus on the importance of taking in His Word each day and drawing from it the things we need to live victoriously, grow closer to Jesus and learn to share His love with those around us. Indeed, God's marvelous Word must become part of the very fabric of our being if we want these things to be true in our lives.

Pastor Rogers had a unique way of helping us take hold of the Bible's truths and incorporate them into our lives. Featured in the front of *The Adrian Rogers Legacy Bible* is his simple yet effective outline for how to assimilate the Word of God. While researching materials to include in that special publication, we were re-energized as we examined so many powerful, biblical messages collected from a lifetime of serving the Lord. But there was so much more material we wished we could include!

Tapestry is the answer to that desire. Through what will become a series of devotional journals, we hope to present a more substantial portion of Dr. Rogers' work, from which you can glean biblical truth to enrich your life. The format for these journals will utilize Dr. Rogers' 5-step process for examining God's Word.

Why 5 Steps?

We feel this wonderfully simple process Pastor Rogers shared is an ingenious way to get the most out of your time spent in God's Word! The principles are basic and memorable, and so effective for helping God's truths to become embedded in your heart and life.

Here's the basic outline for this powerful approach to studying God's Word:

When you get ready to read the Word of God, first **pray over it.** Ask God to teach you. Say, "Dear God, open my eyes. Move my heart. Give me understanding as I read Your Word."

Then **ponder it.** When looking at a passage, ask these six questions:
1. Is there a promise to claim?
2. Is there a lesson to learn?
3. Is there a blessing to enjoy?
4. Is there a command to obey?
5. Is there a sin to avoid?
6. Is there a new thought to carry with me?

Put it in writing. Have a pen and paper ready to write down the things God is showing you. Expect God to reveal essential truth to you and be ready to record it!

When God teaches you a truth, it is vitally important that you **practice it.** Be quick to obey what you are shown and find ways to implement that truth in your daily life.

Next, **proclaim it.** God doesn't just give you knowledge for your own edification, but to share with others. The more of the Bible you give away, the more it sticks to you!

We've taken these steps and incorporated them into the devotional studies you'll find beautifully presented within this journal.

How to Use Tapestry

Each day of study in *Tapestry: Faith & Forgiveness* follows the helpful 5-step format for taking the Word of God into your life.

Pray over it

Before you begin each study, you'll be reminded to pause for a brief **prayer** asking for God's cleansing and for the ability to receive what He wants to teach you. You can use your own words; this is just a starting point to help you consecrate this time to Him.

> Focus my heart and mind on what You want to reveal to me, Lord.

Ponder It

Next is the featured Scripture with some words in bold to emphasize portions of the verses which will be highlighted in that particular study. As you meditate on God's Word and read Dr. Rogers' insights, keep those six "Is there a..." questions in mind to help you **ponder** what message is there for you.

> For I say, **through the grace given to me**, to everyone who is among you, **not to think of himself more highly than he ought** to think, but to **think soberly**, as God has dealt to each one a measure of faith.
> ROMANS 12:3

With a renewed mind, there are several ways we may think of ourselves. This verse gives us the dimensions of a healthy self-image.

Put it in writing

Now, get ready to **put into writing** what the Holy Spirit is revealing to you, personally! The first question on the facing page will always prompt you to record what you've discovered as you've pondered the Scripture and lesson, applying the six "Is there a..." questions.

Practice it

In the next space provided for writing, you'll be prompted to record ways you can incorporate the truths you've just been shown into your own life and begin to **practice** them. This is a great way to hold yourself accountable for acting upon what God has revealed to you, purposing that you will respond with obedience to the truth you've received.

> What lessons did you find here today about genuine humility and the value of a proper self-image?
> _____
> _____
> _____
> _____
> _____
>
> Do you ever find yourself wavering toward either false pride or false humility? What are some specific things you can do to avoid these faulty ways of thinking and think in a "sober" (mind-saving) way?
> _____
> _____

Proclaim it

Lastly, you can contemplate ways to share the new knowledge God has given you. Anticipate how you can **proclaim** His truth to friends, co-workers, family members, loved ones—whomever God brings across your path!

We truly believe applying this simple yet powerful method to your Bible study times will make God's Word come alive in your heart and life!

Abbreviations for the Books of the Bible used in Tapestry: Faith & Forgiveness

Old Testament

Gen.	Genesis	Ecc.	Ecclesiastes
Exo.	Exodus	SOS	Song of Solomon
Lev.	Leviticus	Isa.	Isaiah
Num.	Numbers	Jer.	Jeremiah
Deu.	Deuteronomy	Lam.	Lamentations
Jos.	Joshua	Eze.	Ezekiel
Jdg.	Judges	Dan.	Daniel
Ruth	Ruth	Hos.	Hosea
1 Sam.	1 Samuel	Joel	Joel
2 Sam.	2 Samuel	Amos	Amos
1 Kng.	1 Kings	Oba.	Obadiah
2 Kng.	2 Kings	Jon.	Jonah
1 Chr.	1 Chronicles	Mic.	Micah
2 Chr.	2 Chronicles	Nah.	Nahum
Ezra	Ezra	Hab.	Habakkuk
Neh.	Nehemiah	Zep.	Zephaniah
Est.	Esther	Hag.	Haggai
Job	Job	Zec.	Zechariah
Psa.	Psalms	Mal.	Malachi
Pro.	Proverbs		

New Testament

Mat.	Matthew	1 Tim.	1 Timothy
Mark	Mark	2 Tim.	2 Timothy
Luke	Luke	Tts.	Titus
John	John	Phm.	Philemon
Acts	Acts	Heb.	Hebrews
Rom.	Romans	Jam.	James
1 Cor.	1 Corinthians	1 Ptr.	1 Peter
2 Cor.	2 Corinthians	2 Ptr.	2 Peter
Gal.	Galatians	1 John	1 John
Eph.	Ephesians	2 John	2 John
Php.	Philippians	3 John	3 John
Col.	Colossians	Jude	Jude
1 Ths.	1 Thessalonians	Rev.	Revelation
2 Ths.	2 Thessalonians		

TAPESTRY

Why Faith & Forgiveness?

Your faith is the measure of your victory, your success—all of the things that grace provides come to us by faith. So it is very, very, very, very important that you learn what faith is.

—Adrian Rogers

Through faith in the finished work of Jesus Christ, we can lay hold of all the riches God's grace affords! (Eph. 2:4-9) Forgiveness is the greatest gift of grace because it removes that which separates us from God: our sin. When we come to Him in repentance and faith, and total cleansing is ours, we are free to live like forgiven saints.

This means we are empowered—and expected—to live the Christian life not by trying, but by trusting. Faith is not only how we receive salvation, it is how we walk, day by day, in grace. It's what allows us to enjoy fellowship with God and follow His plan for our lives unhindered by guilt, bitterness or uncertainty. Faith enables us to rest in God's promises in difficult times and look to a better future, confident of His ultimate purposes. Only by faith can we extend forgiveness to others, share God's truth, and leave a godly legacy.

These are just some of the essential truths Pastor Rogers sought to convey as he emphasized throughout his ministry the importance of learning to live by faith. He taught us that, "*The Word of God is translated into faith in our lives when we hear it, believe it, and act upon it.*" And that's exactly what these studies are designed to help you do.

By exploring the "Foundations for Our Faith" in Romans, examining the "Champions of Faith" in Hebrews, and delving into many other Bible passages, Dr. Rogers presented invaluable insights on how to live by faith. We pray the selections we've provided here will help you learn about a way of life that lets you get to know your Savior intimately, teaches you to rely upon His specific promises and purposes for you, and prepares you to one day meet Him face to face! As the tapestry of your life unfolds, may you begin to see the wonders of living each day, moment by moment, a life of faith and forgiveness.

Tapestry

Faith & Forgiveness

Show me, Lord, how to live each day like I've been forgiven.

*But to him who...**believes on Him** Who justifies the ungodly, **his faith is accounted for righteousness**, just as David also describes the blessedness of the man to whom God imputes righteousness apart from works: "Blessed are those whose lawless deeds are **forgiven**...to whom **the Lord shall not impute sin**."*

ROMANS 4:5-8A

God has never imputed sin to one of His children...and He never will. Some people say, "If you sin after you get saved, won't you lose your salvation?" What do they mean, *if*? There's not one person who hasn't sinned after being saved. None of us should trust the best fifteen minutes we've ever lived to get us to heaven! Especially when we understand the Bible's definition of sin: "...whatever is not from faith is sin" (Rom. 14:23) and "Therefore to him who knows to do good and does not do it, to him it is sin" (Jam. 4:17).

Every day, every one of us would have to admit we've failed in some way. But put this down big, plain and straight: if you've repented of your sin and trusted Jesus Christ to save you, you are righteous in God's sight and you are a saint of God! (2 Cor. 5:21) It's imperative to understand that—because until you see who you are, you're not going to live up to your title. Your behavior comes from your concept of who you are. And when you truly see that you're the righteousness of God in Christ, then you'll begin to behave that way.

You should take God's Word and get an accurate perspective of yourself: recognize your righteousness. And realize that your righteousness does not relate to your works at all. It relates to your faith in the Lord Jesus Christ. Instead of sin, you're imputed righteousness. God puts it on your account and it comes to you through what Jesus did on the cross—it is grace all the way! By grace through faith you have become the righteousness of God. (Eph. 2:8-9) So *when* you fail, do confess your sin. But also remember to profess your righteousness. Learn to live every day like you've been forgiven and sainted...because you have!

What new thoughts did you find here about sin, righteousness and who you are in Christ?

_____
_____
_____
_____
_____
_____

Do you ever let your failures keep you from seeing yourself as God sees you? How can these truths help you to avoid such misconceptions?

_____
_____
_____
_____
_____
_____

How could recognizing your righteousness help you when sharing God's truth with others?

_____
_____
_____
_____
_____
_____
_____

Thank You, Lord, for blessings passed on through faithful living!

Behold, **thus shall the man be blessed who fears the Lord**...*may you see the good of Jerusalem all the days of your life. Yes,* **may you see your children's children**. *Peace be upon Israel.*

Psalm 128:4-6

This psalm speaks of the lasting impact a person of faith can have—even leaving as part of their legacy a healthy nation. But perhaps even sweeter is the thought of a personal heritage. The delightful idea conveyed here is of children living in peace because of the legacy of a godly granddaddy.

Singer-songwriter Bill Gaither has a family story that illustrates this beautifully. As newly married school teachers in a small town, he and Gloria didn't have much money, but saved up hoping to buy a bit of land and build a house. They found the perfect spot, but it belonged to a retired banker known for holding onto his property. Though they took their young daughter and went to this man as a nice little family, he had no intention of selling. Until he took note of Bill's name and asked, "Was your granddad Grover Gaither?" When Bill affirmed he was, the old banker said: "He used to work for me. I've never seen a harder working, more faithful man. Son, you came from good stock. Let me think on it. Come back later."

The old man not only sold them the land, he gave them an incredible deal! The Gaithers built there and began planting trees, each year adding more. One day, Bill and his grown son were walking on the property, taking in its beauty. His son asked, "Dad, how did we ever get such a nice place?" Bill had the joy of telling him, "Son, it's because my granddad, your great-granddaddy, was a good and faithful man that we're walking out here today."

You too can leave a legacy, no matter what kind of home you came from. You can say, "By the grace of God, I'm going to be a godly parent and see my children's children loving, serving and praising the Lord!" How we need God-fearing, hard-working fathers and mothers—people of faith who will love each other and lovingly lead their children.

What did you find in Psalm 128 that might be a blessing for you to claim regarding your own family or your personal legacy?

_____
_____
_____
_____
_____
_____

Whether or not you are a parent, you can have a lasting impact on those around you. What could you be doing each day to enrich the legacy you'll leave?

_____
_____
_____
_____
_____
_____

The greatest thing you can pass on to someone else is a faithful testimony of Jesus Christ. Think specifically of a person you could share with today and how you can tell them what He's done in your life.

_____
_____
_____
_____
_____
_____

Thank You, Lord, for continual cleansing!

*If we **confess** our sins, **He is faithful** and just **to forgive us** our sins and to **cleanse us** from **all** unrighteousness.*

1 John 1:9

God knows that when we're saved we don't become sinless—and He made provision for that reality! In the Greek this word *cleanse* means "continues to cleanse" or "continually cleanses." We know from observation, from what the Bible teaches and from personal experience that Christians can sin. Most of us probably sin far more than we even realize every day.

And sin in the life of a Christian causes suffering and great loss, which is why the Holy Spirit will convict you of sin so you can confess it, be made clean again and enjoy fellowship with God. Now the devil will try to drive a wedge of guilt between you and God by accusing you of sins that have already been forgiven and forgotten. (Heb. 8:12) But the Holy Spirit will never bring up sin that has already been dealt with. He only convicts legitimately and specifically in order to lead you to confession and forgiveness, joy and happiness.

When the Spirit speaks to your heart, pointing out things you did or failed to do, just bring those things to the Lord and He will cleanse you. But you must do more than admit your sin...you must confess it, which means agreeing with God about that sin. You view that sin as God views it—a wrong and hurtful thing which needs to be purged from your life—and take sides with Him against it.

This word *confess* is in the present tense. That means confession is to be our continual habit. We should just go through life, day by day, and the minute we're aware of any sin in our lives, confess it completely. Name your sins one by one as the Spirit convicts you and do so confidently. You don't have to beg or plead. Jesus died for you. And you can trust God will be faithful to His Word, continually forgiving any and **all** sins you confess, wiping the slate clean and leaving nothing but His righteousness in you!

If you feel comfortable listing some of the things God has forgiven in your life, you can thwart satanic accusation by turning these back to God as praise and pointing the devil to your divinely clean slate!

_____
_____
_____
_____
_____
_____

What are some things you could do to help make confession your continual habit?

_____
_____
_____
_____
_____
_____

Do you know someone who could be encouraged by what you've learned today? Consider how you might share these truths with them.

_____
_____
_____
_____
_____
_____

Lord, be my sustenance as I walk day by day in faith.

Then the LORD said to Moses, "Behold, I will rain **bread from heaven** for you. And **the people shall go out and gather** a certain quota every day, **that I may test them**, whether they will walk in My law or not."

EXODUS 16:4

When God miraculously sent manna for the children of Israel while they were in the wilderness, it was not only to nourish them but also to test their faith. Each morning they went out to gather the heavenly bread, they demonstrated their reliance upon Him. Manna is a picture of Jesus Himself. This pure white, sweet substance (v. 31) came to them from heaven in abundance—more than they could gather!

God has made perfect, plenteous provision for all of your needs before you even know you have them! (Mat. 6:8, Php. 4:19) And how you feed on Jesus daily is your faith test. It shows your dependence upon the Lord. If you don't have a quiet time, you'll be miserably self-sufficient and you will have a weak faith.

This test for the Israelites also dealt with their appetite. It's true that you are what you eat and you eat what you are. That is, what you desire to eat says so much about you. If you have an inordinate appetite for television or novels, for movies or music or some other tantalizing item on the world's menu, it reveals a lot about the true hunger of your soul. The Israelites remembered the decadent fare of Egypt and complained, "We don't want heaven's bread. We want earth's garlic!" (Num. 11:5-6) Are you like them? Or do you have an appetite for the things of God?

Your quiet time—or lack thereof—shows your dependence on God, your desire for God and your devotion to God. When Jesus compared Himself to manna and talked to His disciples about feeding on Him, many turned away and no longer followed Him. (John 6:26-66) The test of your love for the Lord is this: do you feed on Him? Are you hungry for Him? Would you say, like the old hymn, "Bread of heaven, feed me till I want no more?"

What is God saying to you about your spiritual diet? How can you respond in obedience to what He's revealed to you today?

_____
_____
_____
_____
_____
_____

If your spiritual hunger is waning, what should you do to revitalize it? Think of how you could you lose those cravings for "worldly things" and develop an appetite for the things of God.

_____
_____
_____
_____
_____
_____

Just think how often the topic of food comes up in your everyday conversation—and consider what you might share with someone about the benefits of a healthy spiritual diet.

_____
_____
_____
_____
_____
_____

Lord, give me faith that amazes You.

*When Jesus heard these things, **He marveled** at him, and turned around and said to the crowd that followed Him, "I say to you, **I have not found such great faith**, not even in Israel!"*

Luke 7:9

How would you like to astound the Son of God? It seems safe to say very few things could surprise Jesus. Yet here was something that made Him marvel: a Gentile demonstrating a profound understanding of principles at the very crux of faith. He had discovered how the kingdom of heaven works. Jesus hadn't encountered this—even among the most devout Jews!

How did this Roman officer gain such godly wisdom? As a military man, he understood authority and the chain of command. He knew that the reason he had authority in the army was because he operated under the authority of his superiors. And he rightly recognized the same was true for Jesus. That's why he sent Jesus a message as He was coming to heal the centurion's dying servant. He said, in effect: "You don't need to come to my house, Jesus. Simply say the word and my servant will be healed. I know it's because you're subject to God the Father that You have power over diseases and death. You have only to give the order and Your command will be obeyed." (vv. 6-8) Jesus just stepped back in amazement and essentially said, "What faith!"

This man had learned one of the greatest spiritual lessons anyone can learn: you will never be "over" unless you're willing to be "under". That's why some of us are always being beaten up by the devil and go limping around with a faith that is battered and bruised. We refuse to have a submissive spirit to the authority God has placed over us and therefore we've lost our authority.

Do you have amazing faith? Faith that is great enough to submit and trust God to be over what you cannot control? Only this kind of faith will open up the wonders of God's kingdom authority in your life.

TAPESTRY

Looking at this centurion's faith, what lessons do you find to help deepen your faith and cause you to examine your position in God's chain of command?

_____
_____
_____
_____
_____
_____

God says we must be under authority to have authority. In what ways have you seen this truth demonstrated in your life?

_____
_____
_____
_____
_____
_____

Think of the various people in authority over you. How do you view them—interact with them—respond to them? What might they be able to learn by observing your faith?

_____
_____
_____
_____
_____
_____

Help me to plant seeds of faith in my life, Lord.

...if you have **faith as a mustard seed**, *you will say to this mountain, 'Move from here to there,' and it will move; and* **nothing will be impossible for you**.

MATTHEW 17:20

A mustard seed is tiny about the size of the period at the end of this sentence. So why would Jesus want us to associate our faith with something so miniscule? He wasn't putting a premium on little faith. He was contrasting something very small (a seed) with something very large (a mountain) to help teach us this valuable truth: **the least amount of faith is greater than the greatest amount of difficulty.**

A mustard seed of faith is greater than a ton of willpower, a mountain of determination or an ocean of scheming. Human ingenuity cannot create a seed; only God can do that. And only He can place in you the faith you need to move mountains. You cannot clench your fist, grit your teeth and say "I'm going to believe." Faith is the supernatural gift of God which He will gladly give to you. But you must open your hand to the seed. He will not place it in a clenched fist. A seed is meant to be sowed. If you will take what He gives you, plant it, act upon it—then it will reproduce and there will be more faith growing in your heart and life. That's the secret of a seed: it can grow and produce more seeds. In one seed are thousands of seeds and in thousands of seeds are millions!

It only takes **one** seed to have mountain-moving power. There are mountains of fear and mountains of sickness; mountains of doubt and of poverty, of temptation and of heartache. No matter what you're facing—God says **nothing** will be impossible for you to overcome. "Nothing." And that's God's Word. Now, that may seem pretty vast—as if God somehow overspoke and we'd better water it down for Him or try to explain it away. Why don't we just **believe it**? Why don't we simply take God at His Word, sow that tiny seed of faith He has given us...and see what grows?

What new thoughts does this lesson bring to you about your faith? *(Do you wonder if you even have a mustard seed's worth?)* Consider what you can do to plant the seeds of faith God gives you and see them grow exponentially.

_____
_____
_____
_____
_____
_____

Think of the mountains you're facing today...do you believe God's promise that *"nothing"* will be impossible for you to overcome? How can you trust Him and act upon that faith?

_____
_____
_____
_____
_____
_____

How could you use the encouraging truths in this lesson to reach out to someone else today?

_____
_____
_____
_____
_____
_____

Faith & Forgiveness

Help me to trust You more, Lord.

Jesus said to him, "If you can believe, **all things are possible to him who believes."** *Immediately the father of the child cried out and said with tears,* **"Lord, I believe; help my unbelief!"***

MARK 9:23-24

This father was facing a mountain of difficulty and he knew his faith was weak. He'd just seen the disciples fail against the demon tormenting his son, (v. 18) He was desperate, and he wasn't sure even Jesus could help. *"If* You can do anything, have compassion on us," he plead. (v. 22) **Even feeble faith can lay hold of a mighty God.**

Jesus had just been on the mountain of transfiguration where He was illumined with power and glory. Now He was in the valley of misery. He'd come down from clouds of splendor to encounter a demon-possessed boy, a broken-hearted father, and disciples who were such miserable failures—He rebuked them for their faithlessness. (v. 19) Jesus spoke, the demon fled, and a grateful father was reunited with his son who was patently, permanently cured. The disciples could have done the same, had they had enough faith.

Ashamed, they came to Jesus privately asking, "Master, why couldn't we do it?" His answer: "Because of your unbelief." (Mat. 17:19-20) They believed in Jesus in a sense, but they were unbelieving believers. They hadn't trusted Him enough to act upon the faith they'd been given. That's why Jesus explained that all you need is a mustard seed's worth of faith and seemingly insurmountable mountains—of despair, disease, even demonism—will flee away. (v. 20)

Now Jesus had been speaking figuratively about mountains and mustard seeds, but He said specifically *"this* mountain." So consider what was on the mountaintop He'd just returned from: the glory of God and a preview of Christ's triumphant return! (Mat. 16:27-28) And in the valley there was despair, defeat and heartache. He was saying, "Get rid of the mountain and bring the power of God from on high down into your lives." If we believe, Jesus promises we can have the power to bring heaven and earth together. *Lord, help our unbelief.*

How can you grasp these powerful promises and gain a mountain-moving, devil-defying faith?

_____
_____
_____
_____
_____
_____

This father could not cure his son, but he had faith enough to bring him to Jesus. Consider how you can do the same for your children or loved ones plagued with problems you can't help them overcome.

_____
_____
_____
_____
_____
_____

Do you know someone who's almost given up hope? What can you share with them about the promises of God that will help renew their faith?

_____
_____
_____
_____
_____
_____

Thank You, Lord, for going before us and for pulling me ever closer to the future and the hope You have for me.

*This **hope** we have as an **anchor of the soul**, both **sure and steadfast**, and which enters the Presence **behind the veil**, where **the forerunner has entered for us, even Jesus**...*

Hebrews 6:19-20

The anchor has long been used as a symbol of the Christian faith. If you visit the garden tomb in Jerusalem, you can see there etched on a back wall what appears to be a faint cross. But look closer and you'll discern the points of an anchor. Someone carved that image there centuries ago to symbolize our faith that is anchored in the finished work of the Lord Jesus Christ.

It has been said that hope is faith in the future tense. The reason for our sure hope is illustrated here when the Bible speaks of Jesus as the forerunner Who has taken our anchor behind the veil. In that day there were no engine-powered boats; ships would enter a harbor either by wind or by oars. There were tides and shoals, weather and waves to contend with. If the water was rough or the wind contrary, maneuvering into a harbor might prove impossible. So a forerunner would go in a smaller boat and attach the ship's anchor to one of the great rocks imbedded along the shore. Then at the proper time, the ship, connected by that sturdy rope anchored securely inside, could be pulled steadily and safely into the harbor.

That's the figure of speech being used here, and entering behind the veil means going inside the Holy of Holies—in heaven! (Heb. 9:24) Doesn't it bless you to know that your anchor is already lodged securely in heaven and you're hooked firmly to it? Life may toss you about. The storms may rage, the breakers roll, and your timbers may creak—but you can trust that your anchor will hold. Jesus has gone before us and fastened it to the very throne of God. We are connected to Him with the rope of our salvation and every day you can just feel the tug as He's inching us closer and closer to the heavenly harbor.

What blessings do you find in considering these nautical—and heavenly—images and thinking about the promises of God?

_____
_____
_____
_____
_____
_____
_____

What truths here could help you as you're contending with current or future storms and difficulties in your life?

_____
_____
_____
_____
_____
_____
_____

Name specific ways you could use the truths from this lesson to encourage another brother or sister in Christ.

_____
_____
_____
_____
_____
_____
_____

Let me love You, Jesus, just for Who You are.

> Now **He could do no mighty work there**, except that He laid His hands on a few sick people and healed them. And **He marveled because of their unbelief**...
>
> Mark 6:5-6

Jesus had been amazed to find great faith in the heart of a Roman centurion—a Gentile. As He entered His hometown of Nazareth, He was once again astonished...but this time by the *lack* of faith among His own people.

Their unbelief was rooted in the fact that they *thought* they knew Him. They knew His family, His work. They said, "Isn't this the carpenter?" (v. 3) And that was, indeed, His occupation. Jesus' public ministry lasted only three years. Most of His life was spent doing carpentry work in a despised city. Nazareth was on the wrong side of the tracks, and to those folks, Jesus was just a hometown boy. They refused to believe in Him because of His humble background.

So why did He come as a common carpenter? Why was He raised in an obscure village? It's all wrapped up in God's plan for us in this matter of faith. You see, God wanted people in that day—and He wants us—to love Jesus not for what He can do, but for Who He is.

If God wanted to prove Himself to us, He could just part the sky, lean in and say, "Boo." There'd be no more unbelievers! But if He did that, we'd be following Him not for Who He is primarily but for what He did. He doesn't want that kind of fellowship. That's why when Jesus came to earth, He laid aside all of the majesty and glory that was His outwardly while maintaining all of the character, beauty, and divinity that was His inwardly. So people might love Him not for what He could do, not for what He had, but for Who He is, in and of Himself.

The people of Nazareth kept themselves from truly knowing Jesus. Because they had a "*what you see is what you get*" mentality, they failed in their faith. And their unbelief fettered the hands that wanted to bless and chained the work of the Lord Jesus Christ.

What mindset or attitude might be keeping you from truly knowing the Lord and enjoying the fellowship He desires to have with you?

_____
_____
_____
_____
_____
_____

Would Jesus be perplexed to find unbelief in your heart today? In what ways might you be keeping Him from working in your life?

_____
_____
_____
_____
_____
_____

Think of Who Jesus is to you and consider how you could share this with someone else to help them know true fellowship with the Savior.

_____
_____
_____
_____
_____
_____

Lord, don't let me limit the mighty things You want to do in my life!

So they were offended at Him. But Jesus said to them, "A prophet is not without honor except in his own country and in his own house." Now **He did not do many mighty works there because of their unbelief.**

MATTHEW 13:57-58

The people in Nazareth missed out on the blessings of God because they limited Jesus by their lack of faith. How could the sovereign, omnipotent Son of God be limited by anything these people did? Well, some divine parameters had already been set when Jesus said, "According to your faith let it be to you" (Mat. 9:29). Jesus Himself dictated the bounds and He stayed within them. He allowed Himself to be limited by their unbelief.

Don't be like these folks and let your feelings keep you from believing the Lord. It was an emotional decision. They were offended—"*Who does He think He is?*" And feelings kept them from faith. If you rely on your emotions to determine what you believe, your fickle feelings will one day betray you.

You also can't rely on appearances. All the Nazarenes could see was "the obvious." They refused to live by anything other than the five senses. But we're to live not by looking "at the things which are seen, but at the things which are not seen" (2 Cor. 4:18). If you can't see it or feel it, if it doesn't measure up within the five senses, just step over into the sixth sense of faith.

And never let your faith be limited by logic. These folks had arrived at what they thought was a logical conclusion: "*He's one of us...we're not much... therefore He can't be much either.*" Now logic is not wrong in the Christian faith. But what we believe transcends logic—it rises higher than reason—and becomes its own best reason as we prove it to be true in our lives day by day.

Don't let your faith be fettered by feelings, altered by appearances or limited by logic. Look to the sure Word of God. Believe on it, act upon it and live by it... and see what mighty works God will be free to do in your life!

What new thoughts come from considering how Almighty God allows Himself to be limited by man's unbelief?

___

What interferes with your ability to trust God on a daily basis? Your feelings? Your senses? Analytical thinking? Ask God to help you identify and eliminate the things that are limiting your faith.

___

How can you help someone else overcome emotions, appearances or skewed logic that may be threatening their faith?

___

Thank You, Lord, for inviting me to come confidently before Your throne of grace today.

---

*If any of you lacks wisdom, let him **ask of God**, Who gives to all liberally...and **it will be given** to him. But let him **ask in faith**, with **no doubting**, for he who doubts is like a wave of the sea driven and tossed by the wind.*

JAMES 1:5-6

Why would we not believe that the God Who invites us to pray stands ready to answer our prayers? Why wouldn't we exercise the faith we've been given and go to Him in confidence to ask for whatever it is we lack?

Well, the devil will certainly try to dissuade us because he's scared of the power of prayer. And he knows he cannot keep God from answering, so he'll try to keep you from asking. He'll do his best to demean you, disturb you, distract you, or just deter you from asking in the way God has told us to—in faith.

Whatever you pray for, if you don't pray with faith, you have no expectation of getting your prayer answered. *Pray, believe, and you'll receive; pray and doubt you'll do without.* It's just that simple. But in order to pray the prayer of faith, you must have a word from God. (Rom. 10:17) You must seek and know His will. "Now this is the confidence that we have in Him, that if we ask anything according to His will, He hears us" (1 John 5:14). The prayer that gets to heaven is the prayer that starts in heaven.

There are some things you can always ask for in faith. You can say, "God, I know it's Your will that I have wisdom. Therefore, I can pray in faith and expect You will hear my prayer." And there are many other things you can confidently ask for. Just get in the Word, get the promises of God, and pray them back to Him! Then you'll have firmness in your prayers—no wavering. You'll be able to say "Lord, You invited me to pray. I'm standing firmly on Your Word. I ask You for faith and I believe You for faith. And I thank You for answering my prayer."

God invites us to claim His promises and confidently ask Him for what we need. Why do you think He commands us not to be doubtful when approaching Him in prayer? [continue reading in James 1:7-8]

_____
_____
_____
_____
_____
_____

We know it is God's will for people to be saved and for Christ to be glorified. What else falls within the category of things you can always pray for in faith?

_____
_____
_____
_____
_____
_____

What promises of God could you be confidently praying for a friend or loved one?

_____
_____
_____
_____
_____
_____

Thank You for giving me Your absolute, infallible truth that I can stand upon as the foundation for my life.

---

*Beloved, while I was very diligent to write to you concerning our common salvation, I found it necessary to write to you exhorting you to **contend earnestly for the faith** which was **once for all delivered** to the saints.*

Jude 1:3

Jude wanted to write about the wonderful things believers hold in common in Jesus. But in his day, as in ours, there was a pressing matter that needed to be addressed. Whether you know it or not, there is a battle for the Bible today. There is a fight for the faith and we need to join in.

"*The faith*" refers to the sum total of truth God has revealed to us—His infallible Word. God has established that there is one faith (Eph. 4:5) and it is a settled communication. It was sent to us by the Holy Spirit through the apostles and prophets and never needs to be revised, updated or upgraded. The Greek here literally means "it is once for all time delivered." We don't need a modern Gospel for a modern age. If it's new, it's not true.

Satan continually tries to corrupt the faith (Jude 1:4) and His deceptions are effective. In far too many churches today the Gospel has been watered down to nothing more than a pallid psychology of how to win friends and influence people. Preachers who have jettisoned the faith sabotage the Savior, spouting postmodern theology that subverts the Bible, humanizes God, deifies man, minimizes sin, glorifies science and glamorizes sex. *It is time to earnestly contend for the faith.*

You do that by first submitting to the faith, crowning Jesus Christ Lord of your life and looking to His Holy Word to direct your steps. Study the faith. You can't contend for anything you don't understand. Know what you believe—and live it. Let this faith show in your everyday life. The Bible is the inerrant, inspired, ever-living Word of God! Stand up for the truth! Defend your faith. Be ready to earnestly fight for what you say you believe in.

How can you obey what the Scripture is urging you to do here? What specific steps do you need to take to join in the earnest fight for the faith?

_____
_____
_____
_____
_____
_____
_____

What challenges to the absolute truth of God's Word do you encounter each day? Think of how you might be more aware of these and prepared to defend against Satan's deceptions.

_____
_____
_____
_____
_____
_____

The real proof that you believe God's truth is when you share it with others. Plan how you will share the faith with someone this week.

_____
_____
_____
_____
_____
_____

Lord, help me to experience transformational faith!

> ...Zacchaeus...**sought to see who Jesus was**...and climbed up into a sycamore tree to see Him...And when Jesus came to the place, He... said to him, "Zacchaeus, make haste and come down, for today **I must stay at your house**."
>
> Luke 19:2-5

Maybe this conjures up memories of the song about a "wee little man" with a funny name. But these verses reveal more to us about this man named Zacchaeus than just his stature. They tell of his faith and how it grew into something transformational.

Zacchaeus was basically a crook who had amassed a fortune by cheating his own people. He was rich and despised. But this self-serving swindler had heard about Jesus...and he wanted to know more. Zacchaeus didn't just want to catch a glimpse of Jesus. He wanted to find out **who Jesus was**. When he went to great *heights* to pursue the truth, his faith went from orthodox to experiential.

Once Zacchaeus acted upon his basic belief that there was something worth looking into about this man called Jesus, it didn't take him long to discover that Jesus Christ is Lord. He quickly moved beyond head knowledge to personal experience: "So he made haste and came down, and received Him joyfully" (v. 6). It's not enough to believe *about* Jesus—you must receive Him.

Jesus went home with Zacchaeus. Far too many people leave their Christ at church on Sunday; He doesn't go home with them. They sit in church, nod their heads and believe the facts. But they don't have experiential faith—the kind of faith that transforms you. Something happened to Zacchaeus. His orthodoxy and experience turned to transformation. Freed from greed and dishonesty, he went from despicable to distinguished. (vv. 8-9)

Do you know what set Christopher Columbus apart from his contemporaries? He was willing to set sail on the basis of his faith. It's not enough for you to simply affirm that Jesus Christ is Lord. Are you willing to act upon your belief? Zacchaeus was...and it transformed his life.

What lessons did you find here about pursuing truth and then acting upon what you learn?

_____
_____
_____
_____
_____
_____
_____

Have you taken Jesus home with you? What evidences of this can be found in your daily life?

_____
_____
_____
_____
_____
_____
_____

How could you use these truths to help someone else realize they need to move beyond orthodoxy to a true personal experience with Jesus Christ?

_____
_____
_____
_____
_____
_____
_____

Please show me how to have the same spirit of forgiveness that You have demonstrated, Lord.

*"...If your brother sins against you, rebuke him; a**nd if he repents, forgive him**. And if he sins against you seven times in a day, and seven times in a day returns to you, saying, **'I repent,' you shall forgive him**."*

Luke 17:3-4

We are to forgive freely—but not if someone hasn't repented. It is immoral to forgive them if they don't repent. God does not forgive without repentance: "Unless you repent, you will all likewise perish" (Luke 13:5). There is no forgiveness without somebody paying a price. And there is no forgiveness without somebody repenting. The person who does the forgiving pays the price. But the one who is forgiven must repent.

That doesn't mean you're to be harsh, hateful or hurtful to someone who has sinned against you. You're still to love them and have about you the spirit of forgiveness.

What is the spirit of forgiveness? That's what Jesus Christ had when they were nailing Him to the cross. But notice that Jesus did not say, "I forgive you." Why? Because those who were crucifying Him had not repented. They were in the very act of their sin. Yet He prayed, "Father, forgive them..." (Luke 23:34). He wanted them to have forgiveness. He compassionately sought their forgiveness, even as they were so harshly abusing Him, sinning greatly against Him! And that is the same attitude we are to have toward any person who has wronged us and not yet repented.

Even before you have the opportunity to forgive, you should have the mindset, the willingness and the desire to forgive. You should want that other person to know the joy and freedom that comes with being forgiven. The attitude of forgiveness will free you. The act of forgiveness will free them. And hopefully one day the attitude can become action when he or she says to you, "I repent. I'm sorry. I was wrong." Then you both can be free...free to live humbly and gratefully in the forgiveness you've been given and likewise granted.

What steps do you need to take to respond in obedience to what God is commanding in these verses?

_____
_____
_____
_____
_____
_____

What opportunities do you have throughout your day to demonstrate love and compassion as Christ did to those who were so egregiously wronging Him?

_____
_____
_____
_____
_____
_____

Is there someone who needs to repent for what they've done to you? Think of how you could be praying for them—and ask God to grant you an attitude of forgiveness specifically toward that person.

_____
_____
_____
_____
_____
_____

Let me cast aside any and everything that hinders my faith in You.

―――※―――

*Therefore we also, since we are surrounded by so great a cloud of witnesses, let us **lay aside every weight, and the sin which so easily ensnares** us, and let us run with endurance the race that is set before us...*

Hebrews 12:1

Hebrews chapter 11 begins to delve into the subject of faith by giving us a definition of what faith is and describing what it does. It goes on to depict what can be accomplished "by faith" through example after example of many heroes of the faith. Then in chapter 12 we begin to see how to develop faith. And the writer begins with the word: "Therefore." It's a signal for us to look back to see what has just been said. It refers us to the word God has given.

God gave Scripture to build faith in you. How do you obtain faith in the first place? You must have a word from God. (Rom. 10:17) And "faith is the substance of things hoped for" (Heb. 11:1) which we know means an assurance of God's promises found in His Word. So when we read all about faith in Hebrews 11, then come to a "*Therefore*" we can understand that God is saying: "*Because of this—believe Me. Trust Me.*" Because of the Word we've been given, we can believe Him. The first step in developing faith is to saturate yourself with Scripture. Soak up God's Truth and see how you will begin to trust Him more and more.

Next, you must be separated from sin. We're given the illustration of a spiritual athlete running the race of faith. And like a runner who wants to achieve optimal speed and agility, we're told to lay aside anything that would slow us down or trip us up. Now some things are just weights. They're not sins in and of themselves, but you should get rid of them because they can hinder you. You wouldn't want to run a race wearing a heavy overcoat. Just take those weighty, cumbersome things that could distract or deter you and put them out of your life. But realize that sin will do more than just weigh you down—it will wrap around you and completely immobilize you. There is nothing more debilitating to a life of faith than hidden sin. You cannot advance in your faith until you're no longer entangled in your sin.

What things do you need to lay aside today in order to run the race of faith optimally? What sins could easily trip you up?

_____
_____
_____
_____
_____
_____

How are you saturating yourself with Scripture? Do you follow a specific plan for memorizing, studying and applying the Word of God to your daily life?

_____
_____
_____
_____
_____
_____

Consider how being saturated with Scripture and separated from sin could help you share God's truth with someone whenever an opportunity arises.

_____
_____
_____
_____
_____

Help me, dear Lord, to keep my eyes on the goal!

Therefore...let us lay aside every weight, and the sin which so easily ensnares us, and let us run with endurance the race that is set before us, **looking unto Jesus, the Author and Finisher of our faith***...*

HEBREWS 12:1-2

The Greek verb translated here "looking unto Jesus" has the literal meaning of "looking away from all else in order to fix one's gaze upon something." It means taking your eyes off everything else and turning them solely to Jesus.

When a runner is in a race, he's not to run looking at the other people. Every coach will tell you that you lose just a split second of timing and equilibrium if you turn your head any other way except directly toward the goal. Keep your eye on the goal. And what is our goal as spiritual runners? Well, Jesus is the Author of our faith. He's the One Who fires the gun to start the race. He's the Finisher of our faith...He *is* the goal. Jesus not only puts you in the race and sustains you as you run, He is also the goal you're running for. Just look to Jesus. The more you see and understand of Him, the more your faith will grow.

Imagine you wanted to cross a bridge that spanned a wide expanse, stretching over a rushing river. But you were afraid because you just didn't know for sure the bridge could hold you up. So you could pace there on the riverbank trying to work up some faith, keep mulling things over in your mind and try to make yourself believe...or you could just observe the bridge. You could look at the bridge and see great semi trucks going over it. You could watch automobiles and people travelling across. Then belief becomes automatic. Your faith comes from just looking at the bridge, watching and observing it.

Faith is the by-product of seeing and understanding Jesus. Get into God's Word and learn Who the Christ of the Scripture is. As you look to the Author and the Finisher of your faith, just push aside anything that dims your view of Him. Determine to run with your eye on the goal—the Savior—because dedication to Him is paramount in the race of faith.

What blessings do you find in knowing that Jesus is the Author and Finisher of your faith—and the One Who sustains you as you run toward Him?

_____
_____
_____
_____
_____
_____

Think of all the things you need to look away from in order to focus solely on Jesus. As you examine your devotion to Him today, you might also consider this: *are you more dedicated to the race or to the Savior?*

_____
_____
_____
_____
_____
_____

How could fixing your focus on Jesus help you to see and understand the needs of others and reach out to them with His love?

_____
_____
_____
_____
_____
_____

May I be activated by Your Spirit today, Lord, and emboldened to step out in faith.

―――◆―――

*Therefore...let us lay aside every weight, and the sin which so easily ensnares us, and **let us run with endurance** the race that is set before us, looking unto Jesus, the Author and Finisher of our faith...*

Hebrews 12:1-2

When you've saturated yourself with Scripture, separated yourself from sin and dedicated yourself to the Savior, you'll be activated by the Spirit. You'll gain the fortitude you need to run the race He has called you to run.

Think of how an Olympic runner develops his or her skills. Not simply by studying books about running but by running. Remember, faith is belief with legs on it. So how are you going to develop your faith? Not just by listening to sermons, reading or studying about faith—but by believing God. Find something you can believe God for and begin to believe Him for that. And then you're going to see yourself growing in faith.

It's interesting to learn how the world's first working railway suspension bridge was built over the Niagara River near Niagara Falls. It began with a kite-flying contest! After several days, a kite was successfully flown across the 800-foot chasm and secured on the other side. A stronger line was then attached to that kite string and pulled across. Successively heavier lines could then be pulled across the gorge until a sturdy metal cable was finally connected. As a result, a mighty bridge was built which for decades supported thousands of tons of weight as trains transported passengers and freight between the U.S. and Canada. But it all started...with just a string.

Why don't you choose to believe God for something today? Just fly that kite of faith and say, *"Lord, You've promised this in Your Word, and I believe You for it..."* Then just keep going. Keep believing God for each step of the race before you and watch your faith grow. See how, as you run, you'll be activated by the Spirit of God—vitalized and invigorated as you press toward the goal!

What can you believe God for today? What are some of His promises that stand out to you?

_____
_____
_____
_____
_____
_____

Where do you find yourself most in need of invigoration on a day-to-day basis? How can you trust God to energize you in this area?

_____
_____
_____
_____
_____
_____

Someone you know may be lagging in their race of faith. What truths could you share with them to encourage them to keep pressing toward the goal?

_____
_____
_____
_____
_____
_____

Thank You for caring enough to plan good things ahead of time for me!

*For by grace you have been saved **through faith**, and that not of yourselves; it is the **gift of God**...For we are His workmanship, created in Christ Jesus **for good works**, which God prepared beforehand that we should walk in them.*

EPHESIANS 2:8, 10

If you keep three prepositions in mind it will keep your theology just as straight as an arrow: by, through and for. We are saved ***by*** grace ***through*** faith ***for*** the purpose of fulfilling the good works God has in mind for us to do.

It is grace that saves; faith simply takes hold of the grace God offers to us. Grace is God reaching down from heaven saying, "I love you. I want to save you." Faith is you reaching up saying, "I believe it and I want to be saved." When God's hand of grace meets your hand of faith, that's salvation.

Even the faith that enables us to believe is the gift of God. We could never conjure it up out of our depraved, devilish, disobedient, dead hearts. (v. 2) God puts the faith in your heart. It is His gift—not only salvation but the faith to receive it. And He gives you the ability to move forward from that initial salvation experience to accomplish the good works He has planned ***for*** you to do.

When God makes you into a new creation (2 Cor. 5:17), He's simply crafting you into what you need to be in order to fulfill His purposes for you. Say you have a nice wooden desk in your home or office. That desk didn't cut itself down in the forest, clean itself into boards, saw itself into appropriate pieces and put itself together. Somebody did all of that—it is someone's workmanship. And the maker of the desk planned beforehand for it to be the useful piece of furniture they had in mind. Why do you do good works? Not in order to be saved—but because you have been saved. Because your Maker decided how you could best be used to accomplish wonderful things ***for*** His kingdom when He looked down the corridors of time and saw that you would, ***through*** His gift of faith, reach out to receive His marvelous grace ***by*** which you would be gloriously saved!

How are you encouraged by the thought of God looking down through time and planning the good things you would do for His kingdom? What other new thoughts are here about God's gifts of grace and faith?

_____
_____
_____
_____
_____
_____

What do you feel God has crafted you to do? How are you acting in faith to use the gifts He has given you?

_____
_____
_____
_____
_____
_____

If you know someone who struggles with a "works mentality," how could you help them discover the joy and freedom of knowing they are God's workmanship?

_____
_____
_____
_____
_____
_____

**Help me to glance at my problems and gaze intently at You, Lord—
that I may see the victory of faith You have for me today.**

By faith *the walls of Jericho fell down after they were encircled for seven days.*

Hebrews 11:30

Jericho was a huge citadel, a formidable city that stood as an obstacle between the people of God and the promises of God. Satan will try to place some seemingly insurmountable barrier in front of you to keep you from the will of God in your life. It could be an unhealthy body, an unhappy marriage, an unholy life; it might be old age, lack of education, past defeats. When faced with your Jericho, you can turn around and go back to die in the wilderness of unbelief...or you can do as Joshua did: confront that fortress by faith and conquer it.

Throughout the book of Joshua you'll find this lesson: victory is not achieved by fighting; victory is received by faith. It is *faith* that links our nothingness to God's almightiness and gives us the power to overcome.

How did Joshua build such victorious faith? He had a face to face encounter with the Lord. (Jos. 5:13-15) He was out looking at Jericho and sizing up his problems when he met the mighty Conqueror Who came not to take sides but to take over. And Joshua fell before Him in reverent submission. Faith always grows as we worship the Lord. Joshua became God-conscious rather than problem-conscious. He gladly placed himself under the Lord's command and complied fully, promptly, gladly and unquestioningly to the instructions he was given.

If you'll let the Commander of the Lord's army take over, opposition will crumble and enemies will be vanquished. It doesn't mean you'll have no more problems. Joshua went on from Jericho to many more battles. The victorious life is not freedom from battles. It's freedom *in* battle. We don't fight *for* victory; we fight *from* victory. When we are following the Captain of our faith, we can go from victory to victory, day by day—praising Him all the way!

What is your Jericho today? What have you learned about how to overcome it by faith?

___

Do you spend more time each day sizing up your problems or gazing at your Savior? Consider also how you typically respond to the Lord's commands—fully, promptly, gladly and unquestioningly...or otherwise?

___

No matter what looms before you, threatening to derail your faith, God is bigger. He is able. How could you help someone understand this truth?

___

Faith & Forgiveness

Lord, show me where I should be offering a victory shout today!

*...Joshua said to the people: "Shout, for the L<small>ORD</small> **has given** you the city..."...And it happened when the people...shouted with a great shout, that the wall fell down flat. Then the people went up...and they took the city.*

J<small>OSHUA</small> 6:16, 20

Joshua told the people of Israel to give a victory shout...before the victory had come. At that moment, they were still staring up at the same gigantic walls they'd been marching around for seven days. Nothing had happened. Yet Joshua didn't say, "Shout, for the L<small>ORD</small> **will give** you the city." He said "the L<small>ORD</small> **has given** you the city." Now that may be poor English, but it's mighty good faith!

Joshua knew the whole time they were marching around Jericho that God had already given them the victory. He told them to shout victory before the victory came so that the promised victory would be real. It was a confession of faith that God would keep His Word.

Joshua wasn't being presumptuous. He could say it because God had already said it: "And the L<small>ORD</small> said to Joshua: 'See! I have given Jericho into your hand...'" (v. 2). Faith is just confessing what God has already said. That's when faith becomes real to you. It is confession that brings possession. When you say it, God ratifies it because He's already said it.

We see this principle in Hebrews 13, which speaks of living a godly and contented life, then says: "For **He Himself has said**, 'I will never leave you nor forsake you.' **So we may boldly say**: 'The L<small>ORD</small> is my helper...'" (vv. 5-6). Faith is boldly saying what God has already said.

Perhaps a person is haunted by the ghost of guilt. But when they read in God's Word that the blood of Jesus Christ cleanses us from all sin (1 John 1:7) they are able to say, "Praise God, on the authority of His Word, I now confess and declare that my sin is forgiven!" And their Jericho of guilt just falls; that citadel of condemnation crumbles because they have learned how to say what God has said and confidently claim the victory by faith.

What promises in the Word of God could you confess today and claim the victory of faith for your life?

_____
_____
_____
_____
_____
_____

Why do you think God wants you to be able to stand boldly on what He has said? How does this show in your everyday life?

_____
_____
_____
_____
_____
_____

How could speaking God's words after Him affect the way you reach out to others?

_____
_____
_____
_____
_____
_____

> May I be a delight to You today, Lord, as we walk Your path together.

> **By faith Enoch was taken away so that he did not see death**, "and was not found, because God had taken him"; for before he was taken he had this testimony, that **he pleased God**.
>
> Hebrews 11:5

Enoch's claim to fame was that he walked with God. (Gen. 5:22, 24) And he walked so closely with God that God took him to heaven without his ever even dying. He was the first astronaut!

Genesis 5 reads a lot like an obituary column, listing person after person in Adam's lineage and when they died. But Enoch's name stands out like a gardenia in this desert of death: "And Enoch walked with God; and he was not, for God took him" (v. 24). Enoch didn't die; he just disappeared. He got an express ride to Glory! We aren't told exactly how it happened, but a little girl in Sunday School put it this way: "God and Enoch were walking side by side and they'd walked one day so long, God said, 'Enoch, we're closer to My house than we are to yours; just come on home with Me.'"

Nothing finer could be said about you than that your faith causes you to walk with God. The Bible only makes that statement about two people: Enoch and Noah. (Gen. 6:9) They walked with God. This speaks of having the most intimate fellowship with the Lord. God created us, loved us, and made a way to save us so we could love Him. He longs for us to walk with Him, spend time with Him—get to know Him in a real and personal way.

A walk is going side by side, hand in hand, enjoying each other's company. Walking with God surely brought Enoch enjoyment—but notice the Bible says *Enoch* pleased *God*. Did you know God enjoys walking with you? "The steps of a good man are ordered by the Lord, and **He delights** in his way" (Psa. 37:23). It pleases God when we walk with Him along the path He has planned for us. Just think: God is delighted with your company! And the more delightful walks you share with Him, the deeper your faith will grow.

Tapestry

Is it a new thought for you that *God* gets enjoyment from walking with *you*? How can you let this concept enhance the intimate times you spend with Him?

_____
_____
_____
_____
_____
_____
_____

God has a plan for your life—He knows what steps you should take to accomplish all you need each day. What can you do throughout your day to be sure you're walking with Him along His perfect path for you?

_____
_____
_____
_____
_____
_____
_____

How could you use these truths to encourage someone else to pursue delightful walks with the Lord and deepen their faith?

_____
_____
_____
_____
_____
_____
_____

May my life be a testimony of Your faithfulness, Lord.

By faith Enoch was taken away so that he did not see death, "**and was not found**, *because God had taken him*"; *for* **before he was taken he had this testimony**, *that he pleased God.*

HEBREWS 11:5

Enoch didn't just stroll along with God for an afternoon. He walked with God for three hundred years. (Gen. 5:22) And he maintained his walk as family man, raising sons and daughters in an evil, lascivious time. If you don't have a faith that works at home—a faith that stands out in an evil age—a faith that sustains you day after day, year after year...then what you have is false. It's not truly faith in the Lord Jesus Christ.

People noticed the reality of Enoch's faith; they saw the testimony of his life. They noticed too when he disappeared! They looked and couldn't find him; it was a mystery to them. There will be a whole generation of people who'll experience this—and it could be this generation. One day they may be looking for us and wondering at the mystery of our disappearance. (1 Ths. 4:16-17) The rapture of the Church is prefigured in Enoch.

Enoch himself prophesied of the end times: "Now Enoch, the seventh from Adam, prophesied...saying, 'Behold, the Lord comes with ten thousands of His saints...'" (Jude 1:14). Isn't it amazing that a man only a few generations from Adam would prophesy about the Second Coming of Jesus Christ? What wonders Enoch's faith enabled him to behold as God walked with him and showed him the mysteries of things to come.

The one thing Enoch didn't see was death. God just took him away to be with Him. People didn't understand what happened to old Enoch who walked by faith. The world won't understand the mystery of the rapture either. But they will be looking for answers. If Jesus were to come today, would you be ready? If He were to call you home, would your testimony be missed? How closely are you walking with the Lord?

As you reflect on those closing questions, consider what lessons God is revealing to your heart and decide how you can act upon them in faith.

_____
_____
_____
_____
_____
_____

We see in Genesis 6:5-7 that Enoch knew the difficulties of trying to live for the Lord and raise a family in an utterly wicked age. Consider how your faith sustains you in today's world and helps you meet life's daily demands.

_____
_____
_____
_____
_____
_____

What could others learn by looking at the testimony of your life? What legacy of faith would you like to leave behind?

_____
_____
_____
_____
_____
_____

Lord, help me to hear the word You have just for me today.

So then **faith comes by hearing**, *and* **hearing by the word of God**.

ROMANS 10:17

If you don't hear God, you'll never have faith. Now the "word" in this verse is not the *logos*, meaning the revelation of the Bible, the written Scripture we would call the Word of God. But it is a different Greek word: *rhema*, which refers to the spoken word. It means "the communication of the Word of God"—when the Holy Spirit delivers a message to your heart?

Not to deprecate the Word of God at all, but it is not the Bible you hold in your hand that's going to give you faith. It is God speaking to you out of that Bible. Your heart needs to receive God's direct communication of the truth He has specifically for you.

You can hear with your ears everything a preacher says or comprehend with your mind all that you read in the Bible and still not have faith. But when God speaks to your heart—that is when the seed of faith is planted within you. And the job of any preacher is not just to teach you some sermon outline. It is to get you to listen to God as He speaks to you. You've got to hear more than a sermon, more than a pastor; you've got to hear God. When you read the Bible, God is going to take a word out of the Word and He's going to put that word in your heart. He's going to be meeting the needs of your heart.

Dwight L. Moody was a man of great faith. But he gave this testimony:

> I prayed for faith and thought that someday faith would...strike me like lightning. But faith did not seem to come. One day I read..."Faith cometh by hearing, and hearing by the word of God." I had up to this time closed my Bible and prayed for faith. I now opened my Bible and began to study, and faith has been growing ever since.

Faith comes from hearing the message God imparts to your heart as you study His Word. He has something special to say to you today, if you will listen.

What blessing do you find in knowing that God has a word He wants to share just with you? What do you hear Him saying to your heart today?

_____
_____
_____
_____
_____

How often have you prayed for faith, but neglected to study God's Word? What more could you do throughout your day to help you meditate on His Word and really listen for the message God is speaking to your heart?

_____
_____
_____
_____
_____

How could you encourage someone else to discover the message God has just for them?

_____
_____
_____
_____
_____

Help me, Lord, to gain the victory You desire for me today.

> Then he said to the king of Israel, "Put your hand on the bow." So he put his hand on it, and Elisha put his hands on the king's hands. And he said, "Open the east window"; and he opened it. Then Elisha said, "**Shoot**"; and he shot. And he said, "**The arrow of the Lord's deliverance**..."
>
> 2 Kings 13:16-17

The aged prophet Elisha was sick and near death and Israel was suffering from constant Syrian attacks. King Joash was heartbroken over the state of his country and the thought of losing their spiritual leader. (v. 14) Elisha's last instruction to him was an interactive victory lesson.

He told the king to take up a bow and some arrows (v. 15)—not as literal weapons for his fight, but to aid in demonstrating the true source of his victory. They speak of the power of God and remind us to take up the weapons He has given us. (2 Cor. 10:4) Joash was then shown his own weakness as the man of God laid his hands upon the king's. Our frail hands must be overlaid by God's omnipotent hand. Even spiritual weapons will not overcome the devil when wielded in our own strength. God does not need our strength. He calls for our obedience.

With God's omnipotence wedded to his obedient weakness, Joash then had to face his fears by opening the window toward the east, where Syria was. Many of us aren't willing to expose the place of our fear and failure. But victory's arrows cannot be shot through closed windows.

What good is it to have the bow and arrow, to have someone's hands over yours to help pull the bowstring and aim through the open window—if you do not let that arrow go? *It is faith that acts and brings the enemy to his knees.* Shooting that arrow into enemy territory was a declaration of war. It was an attitude of faith and an affirmation of victory. When that arrow was put into motion, so was the arrow of the Lord's deliverance. God will equip, strengthen and direct you; He'll usher in His powerful forces to secure your victory...but *you* must release the arrow by faith.

Is something defeating you? Tell God where you need deliverance and ask Him for the faith to take that first step and release the arrow that leads to victory.

___

The rest of this passage shows how Joash limited his victory by responding half-heartedly to God's commands for him. (vv. 17-19) Plan for how you can have total victory as you wholeheartedly respond to what God is telling you.

___

How might it affect you to think of God's hands over your hands as you're sharing His Word, speaking about what He has done in your life or reaching out to someone with His love?

___

Faith & Forgiveness

May I cling to Your promises, Lord, and always have faith that You will keep Your Word.

---

*By faith Joseph, when he was dying, **made mention of the departure of the children of Israel**, and gave **instructions concerning his bones**.*

Hebrews 11:22

It seems odd that this is the one thing God would highlight from the life of Joseph to illustrate his great faith. It may also seem strange that Joseph was so concerned about what would happen to his bones after he was gone. But within Joseph's instructions was an assertion of what he knew God was going to do—something he didn't want to miss out on.

Joseph told the children of Israel to carry his bones with them when they left Egypt for the Promised Land. (Gen. 50:24-25) Twice in this passage Joseph affirmed what God would "surely" do. His confident faith was rooted in the Word of God. He knew they were going to leave Egypt because God had told Abraham that the Jews were going to be captives for 400 years and then they would come out. (Gen. 15:13-14)

But it didn't seem like they were going to leave. When Joseph said this he was Prime Minister of Egypt. The Israelites weren't slaves but were in a place of great favor. In fact, they'd left Canaan because of a famine, so why would they want to return? From all appearances there was no reason they should go. But faith doesn't depend upon appearances. And the centuries cannot erode the promises of God. Joseph was clinging to the Word of God and his faith was undiminished. He didn't speculate about *if* they were going; he said, "**When** you go, take me!" Time and circumstances seemed against it, but God's Word stood firm. He would fulfill to the letter what He had promised hundreds of years before.

Joseph had a promise from the Lord and he acted on it. He said, "God is going to keep His Word; and when He does, I want to be a part of it." That is faith. How badly do you want to be in on what God is going to do?

Reflect on some of God's promises to you. Now consider how you are acting upon those and making plans to be part of what you believe He is going to do.

_____
_____
_____
_____
_____
_____

Do you trust God to keep His Word, no matter what circumstances seem to say? What prophecies are you looking for Him to fulfill and how are you praying for those to come to fruition?

_____
_____
_____
_____
_____
_____

Joseph's confidence must have engendered faith in those around him. How might you do the same as you actively anticipate the fulfillment of His promises?

_____
_____
_____
_____
_____
_____

Help me to live out my faith by showing Your love to others, Lord.

***Receive one who is weak in the faith**, but not to **disputes over doubtful things**...each of us shall **give account of himself to God**. Therefore let us not judge one another anymore, but rather resolve this, **not to put a stumbling block...in our brother's way**.*

Romans 14:1, 12-13

The early church was struggling because some were weak in the faith and some were strong. The weaker believers were rigid, refusing to take part in certain things. The stronger Christians knew these particular things weren't wrong in and of themselves, so they did them. Some were being judged for the liberties they took, some despised for their narrow-mindedness. They were divided...over dietary items and days of worship. (vv. 2-6)

One of Satan's chief tools is disunity in the Body of Christ. He would love to divide us over incidentals. A centuries-old theological motto applies here: "In essentials, unity; in nonessentials, liberty; in all things, charity." We should focus on being united over the fundamentals, the main one being: *Jesus Christ is Lord.* Embrace anyone who names Jesus as Lord, even if they are weak in their faith, because they are your brother or sister in Christ.

Know that all Christians have freedom to choose in nonessential matters. But we cannot violate our conscience. If you believe something is wrong, or if you're unsure it's right for you, leave it alone. If it's not of faith it is sin. (vv. 22-23) Always act in faith, for we will all answer to God for our actions (vv. 10-12), including how they affect others. (v.15) If it grieves someone to see you do something, or it might cause someone to fall into sin, just abstain out of love for that person.

Our job is to build up one another. (v. 19) We must be careful not to judge because we don't have all the facts. *In essentials, unity*: Jesus is Lord. *In nonessentials, liberty*: give others the freedom to act as they see fit and be ready to answer for your own actions before God. *In all things, charity*: we are to love one another as Christ has loved us.

As Christians, we are bound together by our common faith—and our faith should dictate our actions. What steps of obedience do you need to take in response to what God has shown you today?

_____
_____
_____
_____
_____
_____

Incredibly, it seems these believers couldn't agree on food and fellowship! What frivolous things do you see dividing people of faith today, and how could you be part of the solution?

_____
_____
_____
_____
_____
_____

In what areas do you have liberty that others might not? What would happen if before taking action you asked, *"Will doing this cause harm to someone else?"*

_____
_____
_____
_____
_____
_____

Thank You, Lord, that I can have a sure faith!

To those who have obtained **like precious faith...grace and peace** *be multiplied to you* **in the knowledge** *of God and of Jesus our Lord, as His* **divine power** *has given to us* **all things** *that pertain to life and godliness...by which have been given to us...* **precious promises***, that through these you may be* **partakers of the divine nature***...*

2 Peter 1:1-4

Peter says all who put their trust in Jesus Christ as Lord and Savior have the same kind of faith: precious, for it was purchased with the precious blood of Christ. (1 Ptr. 1:18-19) This precious faith will give you confidence because it is rooted in knowledge. You can be a "know so" Christian—sure that you are sure of your salvation.

The word translated *knowledge* here is *epignósis*, and it means: "knowledge gained through first-hand relationship." It is experiential. Your faith is based on that kind of personal knowledge. (John 17:3) We know Jesus by faith; but when we get to heaven, we're going to meet Someone face to face that we've already known heart to heart.

Pardon comes through the knowledge of Jesus Christ. The only way your sins can be forgiven is for Christ to be your Savior. (1 Ptr. 1:1) And peace comes—but the Bible is very exact. Always it is grace and then peace, because you cannot know the peace of God until you've experienced the grace of God when your sins are pardoned.

We have power through the knowledge of Jesus. (2 Ptr. 1:3) Everything you need to live the Christian life, you already have if you have Jesus. It is all in Christ and He is in you. And this first-hand knowledge allows you to partake of His divine nature in you! (v. 4) The Bible is full of precious promises. But if you don't know them, you can't lay hold of them and have the victory God wants you to have. You're not just meant to know *about* these things but to know them experientially. The faith that makes you sure is the faith that knows.

What truths did you find here that will help you have assurance, have more peace and lay hold of more of God's precious promises?

How would your life be different if you faced each day truly confident that you already have all you need to live the Christian life?

What did you learn that could help you reach out to someone of like faith who might be struggling with assurance?

May I be diligent to add to the precious faith You have provided, Lord.

―――※―――

But also for this very reason, **giving all diligence, add to your faith** virtue, to virtue knowledge, to knowledge self-control, to self-control perseverance, to perseverance godliness, to godliness brotherly kindness, and to brotherly kindness love.

2 PETER 1:5-7

Once you become a partaker of the divine nature, you must continue to grow your faith. If you're not growing, you're disobeying because this book ends with a command to "grow." (2 Ptr. 3:18) Growth is your responsibility. *Giving all diligence* means you don't let anything keep you from growing your faith by adding these seven qualities:

Virtue, meaning strength and moral excellence; this word was used when something was fulfilling the purpose for which it was made. Practical **knowledge** is gained as you study the Bible and learn to apply God's truth to your life. Next is **self-control**—over your temper, sexual desires, appetite, sleep habits. You can be saved, but if you have no control, you're not a growing Christian.

And then **perseverance**, withstanding persecution. (2 Tim. 3:12) This also applies to suffering irritations like traffic jams, lost keys or late flights! To endure patiently, just praise God in every trial. Because nothing but good comes from Him; and if Satan's behind the trouble, he may stop when he sees he's causing you to praise God!

Next add **godliness**, which is simply God likeness. Just let the light of Jesus shine through you and glorify God. Then **brotherly kindness**, love for the brethren. And the epitome of these qualities is agape **love**—which goes to all people without exception. You don't have to like what they're doing, but you can actually love the drug dealers, pornographers, rapists and murderers. Love says, "I will not give you what you deserve but what you need." That's what Christ did for us. No wonder growing to this level of maturity in our faith requires **all diligence**!

TAPESTRY

Looking at these seven qualities that are to be added to your faith, how well are you following God's command to "grow"?

_____
_____
_____
_____
_____

Consider placing these where you can review them daily, asking: *Am I growing in virtue? Knowledge? Self-control? Perseverance? Godliness? Brotherly love? Agape love?* (Begin by writing them out here and evaluating.)

_____
_____
_____
_____
_____

If you think someone is not worthy of your love—remember, neither were you when God loved you. (1 John 4:11) How do you think you can grow to the point where you can truly love everyone, without exception?

_____
_____
_____
_____
_____

May I always live in gratitude for what You have done for me, Jesus.

For if these things are yours and abound, **you will be neither barren nor unfruitful** *in the knowledge of our Lord Jesus Christ. For he who lacks these things is* **shortsighted***, even to* **blindness***, and has* **forgotten** *that he was* **cleansed from his old sins***. Therefore, brethren,* **be even more diligent to make your call and election sure...**

2 PETER 1:8-10

Did you know that you can be saved and almost forget it? You can become blind to God's marvelous work of grace in your life. You can forget your calling and be an ineffective and unproductive Christian... if you're not diligently devoted to growing your faith. But if you have a faith that knows and a faith that grows, you will have a faith that shows!

Cultivating the qualities Peter gave us in verses 5-7 brings fruitfulness, and you'll find that you are fulfilling what you've been called to do. Jesus said: "You did not choose Me, but I chose you and appointed you that you should go and bear fruit, and that your fruit should remain" (John 15:16). You can produce lasting results for the kingdom of heaven if these qualities abound in your life.

The believer who lacks these things can't see afar; he has no vision for eternal rewards. Unable to see his future and blinded to the glory that belongs to the children of God, he's no longer grateful for what Christ has done for him. *You can get so bogged down with the cares of this world that you fail to see the glories of heaven toward which you are headed and you forget the pit of hell from which you were taken.* Thank God every day for what He has done for you. Never lose sight of how He has saved you by His grace and keeps you day by day.

God never loses His perspective. When Peter says to "make your call and election sure," that doesn't mean from God's point of view. He knows these things are already settled in eternity. You're to make it sure from *your* viewpoint so you can have a confident faith—a faith that knows and grows and **shows** as you live a fulfilling life of gratitude, vision and fruitfulness!

TAPESTRY

Take a moment to reflect on what you were and/or what you *could be* without Christ. Do you truly live a life of gratitude to Him? What is God asking you to do today in response to this lesson?

_____
_____
_____
_____
_____
_____

Are you bearing fruit? How are you furthering the cause of Christ? Are people coming to Him and/or do believers love Jesus more because of you?

_____
_____
_____
_____
_____
_____

What do you think shows through most in your life? What qualities do you most need to develop in order for people to be drawn to Christ in you?

_____
_____
_____
_____
_____
_____

Thank You for complete cleansing, forgiveness and restoration!

> Then **Abram went up from Egypt**...to the place where his tent had been **at the beginning**, between Bethel and Ai, to the place of **the altar** which he had made there **at first**. And there Abram c**alled on the name of the L**ORD.
>
> GENESIS 13:1, 3-4

Bethel is where Abraham first called on the name of the LORD. (Gen. 12:8) He worshiped there in the place whose name means "House of God." Now, through a series of compromises and bad choices, he'd had a relapse in faith. He'd gotten far away from God's fellowship and God's will for his life. How could his broken faith be repaired?

First, there was repentance. He forsook Egypt. In the Bible, Egypt is synonymous with sin. You cannot get right with God and remain in Egypt. If there is some sin in your life that's stultifying your faith, repent of it. The most miserable person on earth is not an unsaved person—but a saved person who is out of fellowship with God. Oh, the misery of believing in God and living in Egypt!

Then there was remembrance. He went back to the place where God was real to Him. Was there ever a time when God was nearer and dearer to you than He is right now? If so, you're backslidden. Just remember how sweet it was when you walked with the LORD. If you feel far away and wonder how you can get back to God...you'll find Him right where you left Him. Go back to your first love.

Abraham went back to the altar. He surrendered everything back to God. And the LORD cleansed him, forgave him and restored his faith. Here's a blessing: you don't find anything about Abraham's failure in the New Testament. You only find that in the Old Testament. God did not remember his sin. God remembered his faith. Isn't God good? When He forgives us, He remembers our sin no more. (Heb. 8:12) So if you've gotten away from God, do what Abraham did. Come out of Egypt. Go back to the altar; give it all back to the LORD. And walk by faith—enjoying sweeter and sweeter fellowship with Jesus each day!

In considering Abraham's faltering faith, did God show you a sin you should avoid or a command you need to obey? What blessings can you enjoy as you think of the restoration of faith?

_____
_____
_____
_____
_____
_____

Think of the happiest, holiest moment you've ever known when God was the most real to you. Is He that real to you right now? How can you maintain a sweet fellowship with Him daily?

_____
_____
_____
_____
_____
_____

What did you learn today that could help you lovingly reach out to someone who needs to come back to God's house?

_____
_____
_____
_____
_____
_____

Let me not underestimate my enemy, but stand in victory, Lord!

---

*Put on the **whole armor of God** that you may be able to stand against the wiles of the devil...**above all, taking the shield of faith** with which you will be able to **quench all the fiery darts of the wicked one**.*

Ephesians 6:11, 16

There is a battle between life and death, light and darkness, heaven and hell. And every Christian is called to be a part of it. Your adversary, the Devil, is a definite fact and a destructive force (vv. 11-12) working strategically to destroy all that is good and holy in your life. He's also a defeated foe, for Satan's back was broken at Calvary. But this makes him dangerously desperate. So you must take up the armor God has provided for your protection in this spiritual battle.

You will need all of this holy armor to defend against the tactics of your enemy. (vv. 13-17) Satan uses lies against you, so put on integrity. He uses lust, so put on purity. He uses discouragement, so put on tranquility. And against Satan's fiery darts of doubt, take up the shield of faith, which is certainty.

Shields in this day were generally large enough to cover the whole body. They were often made of wood overlaid with leather and could be dipped in water before battle to extinguish the flaming darts which were common artillery. When a barrage of these reed-like projectiles was released, they might not look particularly dangerous, but they were deadly incendiary devices which splattered flammable liquid on whatever they struck and set it ablaze. Satan constantly fires subtle darts of doubt, hoping to lodge them in your heart and mind. What may seem like paltry little uncertainties can be fiery ammunition from the very pit of Hell that will destroy you if not deflected or extinguished by your faith.

To take this shield "above all" means to hold it over all the other equipment that is already in place. The shield could be maneuvered to cover any vulnerability and thwart attacks from all directions. Though your armor might develop a chink, or some vital piece of equipment get lost in the heat of battle, you can hold fast to God's over-arching protection. And every fiery dart will be quenched in that shield of faith.

Does Satan try to make you doubt God's goodness? His mercy? His love? If you have areas prone to enemy attacks, take time to reinforce your faith by writing out specific attributes of God along with verses related to those qualities.

_____
_____
_____
_____
_____
_____

Read Ephesians 6:13-18; identify each piece of armor and weapon we have and see how that translates practically to God's protection and power in your life.

_____
_____
_____
_____
_____

What truths did you discover here that you could share with a friend or loved one struggling with uncertainties in their life?

_____
_____
_____
_____
_____

Faith & Forgiveness

Help me see every "impossible situation" through eyes of faith.

*By faith Moses, when he was born, **was hidden** three months **by his parents, because they saw** he was a beautiful child; **and they were not afraid** of the king's command.*

HEBREWS 11:23

Their names aren't even mentioned here. Yet God placed this couple in His hall of fame among other renowned heroes of the faith—like their son Moses. In the world's eyes, Amram and Jochebed may have been just helpless Hebrew slaves. But they shook the world by raising a child for God. And that's a task which cannot be done apart from faith.

Amram and Jochebed saw through eyes of faith that God had given them a very special child. They knew God had promised to bring His people out of bondage. Maybe His Word resonating in their hearts told them their baby was "the one" God would use to lead them out of Egypt. God has a plan for each precious little one. Parents, see your children as unique gifts from God and relish the joy of raising them by faith, according to the vision God gives you for your child.

It won't be easy in today's world. But Moses' parents faced perilous times. Pharaoh ordered the murder of all newborn male Hebrew babies. (Exo. 1:22) Amram and Jochebed saw this as a spiritual conflict and were not afraid to stand against the evil of their day. Don't be afraid to take a position of faith for your kids. There are times when you must believe God for your children. To the man who wanted healing for his demon-possessed son, Jesus said, "All things are possible to him who believes" (Mark 9:23). The burden to believe was placed on the parent, not the child. That boy was not in a position to believe at that particular time. He needed someone to have faith for him.

Moses' parents acted by faith and did what they could to preserve the life of their child. Then they trusted God to do the rest. By God's providence, Moses would grow up in the palace as Pharaoh's grandson. But not before he was nurtured in a household of faith where his own parents could pour God's lasting truth and love from their hearts into his.

TAPESTRY

Psalm 112:1-2 contains a promise you might claim for your children and pray for them—or for any child who is near and dear to your heart. Write out at least one thing that is special to you about each child.

_____
_____
_____
_____
_____
_____

Looking to God's promise gave Amram and Jochebed the courage they needed to take action. What do you need courage to stand against today? Are you facing any "impossible situations" that require a vision of faith?

_____
_____
_____
_____
_____

Does someone need you to have faith for them right now? How can you believe God for that person and help them look to His promises to gain their own vision of faith?

_____
_____
_____
_____
_____

Faith & Forgiveness

May I live a life of faith that embodies the richness of Christ.

> *By faith Moses*, when he became of age, **refused** to be called the son of Pharaoh's daughter, **choosing** rather to suffer affliction with the people of God than to enjoy the passing pleasures of sin, **esteeming** the reproach of Christ greater riches than the treasures in Egypt; for **he looked to the reward.**
>
> Hebrews 11:24-26

Faith was in the heart of Moses because it was in the heart of his parents. Though he was brought up in the Egyptian culture, he had an unmistakable, unshakeable faith in Almighty God when he became a young adult. Amram and Jochebed implemented this biblical principle: "Train up a child in the way he should go and when he is old he will not depart from it" (Pro. 22:6). Training is more than teaching. It is disciplining, shaping—instilling by instruction and example solid values your children can build their lives upon.

Vicious forces are vying for the hearts and minds of our children, trying to snatch away their allegiance, love, and even their souls. Beware the kidnapper, Satan himself, and the methods he uses: liberalism in the church, humanism in schools, paganism in society and especially materialism in the home. Egypt was the reigning dynasty of that day and Moses was in line for the throne. Power, privilege and prestige were his. Yet he chose suffering with God's people over the luxuries of a royal court—because he'd been shown the riches of Christ.

A desire for Jesus was instilled in Moses when he was young. When it came time to choose, he looked at Egypt's enticements and evaluated what he knew. It turned out his parents put something in him that all his Egyptian professors could not take away. He refused the lavish, empty life of royalty in favor of the greater, eternal reward. Many parents today are telling their kids: "There's no lasting pleasure in what the world offers." But what are we giving them that's **better**? Try to take a nasty bone away from a dog and you'll get bitten. But lay a juicy steak on the ground and he'll drop that bone. We have to show young people the beauty and riches of Christ so they can esteem and say "Yes, **that's** what I want!"

Think of some spiritual truth taught to you by your mom or dad—or someone who poured God's love into your life. How is that truth affecting your value system today?

_____
_____
_____
_____
_____
_____

How are you living a life of faith before your kids, family, loved ones or friends that exemplifies the riches and beauty of Christ?

_____
_____
_____
_____
_____
_____

Even if you aren't a parent, God may want to use you to speak truth and love into the life of a child or young person. Consider what kind of influence you could have and think of ways you might reach out to impact this generation for Christ.

_____
_____
_____
_____
_____
_____

I thank You that forgiveness is a matter of mercy, not mathematics.

*Then Peter came to Him and said, "Lord, **how often shall my brother sin against me, and I forgive him?** Up to seven times?" Jesus said to him, "I do not say to you, up to seven times, but up to **seventy times seven**."*

Matthew 18:21-22

Jesus was not telling Peter to keep a tab and forgive someone up to 490 times, but not beyond that. His expression meant to extend forgiveness as many times as someone comes to you asking for it—out into infinity. Just forget the arithmetic. Forgiveness is a matter of the heart, not the head. And you're to forgive others the same way God forgives you.

When God forgives us, it's *always* **the first time** because all the other sins are buried in the grave of His forgetfulness. So *every* time you're forgiving a person who comes to you—it's **the first time**. All of the other times are gone. You don't keep records but forgive as many times as needed.

If you do not forgive, you'll be like the wicked servant in the parable Jesus told next. (vv. 23-35) This man begged mercy from his king and was forgiven an enormous debt. He then cruelly mistreated a fellow servant who owed him but a small amount and had the man imprisoned. Hearing this, the king reinstated the servant's immense debt and sent him to be tortured. Jesus said God the Father will do the same to us if we refuse to forgive our brother. God wants us to value the forgiveness we've received and let that motivate us to act in kind toward others.

Think of your sin as a debt you owe God. You're also indebted to Him because He created you and takes care of you day by day, providing everything from the air you breathe to the food you eat. We use His resources and abuse His love, and we owe Him an inestimable sum we cannot begin to pay. But thank God He has fully paid this debt for us! There's no such thing as free forgiveness. The king did not simply overlook his servant's huge debt. He **absorbed** it. It cost him dearly to forgive. God does not overlook your sin. He has paid for it. With the silver of His tears and the gold of His blood, Jesus purchased our redemption.

What did you learn about God's mercy and justice in this lesson? Did you discover any new thoughts about wiping the slate clean and what it truly means to forgive…and forget?

_____
_____
_____
_____
_____
_____

Think of how you could go through your day with a keener awareness of all the ways God provides for you and cares for you—and how you might "give back" to Him in the form of thankfulness and praise for these things in your life.

_____
_____
_____
_____
_____
_____

Using the truths in today's lesson, how would you encourage someone to keep extending forgiveness even if they're finding it difficult to do so?

_____
_____
_____
_____
_____
_____

Thank You, Jesus, for willingly paying redemption's price!

Looking unto Jesus, the Author and Finisher of our faith, **Who for the joy that was set before Him endured the cross, despising the shame**, *and has sat down at the right hand of the throne of God.*

HEBREWS 12:2

On the cross Jesus was paying the debt that you and I owed. God could not simply cancel the debt until He first paid it, because He is a righteous and holy God. Do you know why He paid that price? It was worth it to Him.

Have you ever noticed that if you pay for something you *really* want, you don't mind paying the price? But have you ever gotten something thinking it was a great bargain and then later regretted buying it? A businessman told about the most expensive suit he ever purchased. He said:

> I bought a suit off the rack knowing I didn't like it, but it was marked down to only $90. I wore it once and never put it on again. It cost me $90 to wear that suit one time—most expensive suit I ever owned!

The bitterness of poor quality lingers long after the sweetness of cheap price has been forgotten. If you buy something and like it and get lots of use out of it, it's worth it. You can say, "Yes, I paid a big price. But look what I got!"

Forgiveness is not cheap. But it's worth what you pay for it. Consider what Jesus paid: He knew He was going to suffer extreme physical anguish and the especially loathsome shame of bearing all of our sins while being executed in the most humiliating and accursed way. (Gal. 3:13) Crucifixion was reserved for the vilest offenders and was intended to disgrace and inflict horrific pain. Yet Jesus went willingly to Calvary and endured unspeakable agonies as He paid with His life for our offenses. What did He get? The joy of making a way for us to be exonerated and join Him at the right hand of the Father for eternity!

There are no bargain pardons. It costs to be forgiven. Yet Jesus' joy increases each time a lost soul by repentance and faith claims that forgiveness for which He paid so dearly.

What new thoughts does this study provoke for you about the price of sin and the cost of forgiveness?

_____
_____
_____
_____
_____
_____

Our lives should reflect our utter gratitude and awe for what Jesus did for us at Calvary. What are you consciously doing to glorify Him and bring His heart joy?

_____
_____
_____
_____
_____
_____

Have you ever felt it was just too costly for you to forgive someone? What joys could you look to in order to find the willingness to pay that price and reach out in love and Christ-like forgiveness?

_____
_____
_____
_____
_____
_____

Help me to be as generous with my forgiveness as You are, Lord.

*"...If your brother sins against you, rebuke him; and if he repents, forgive him. And **if he sins against you seven times in a day, and seven times in a day returns to you, saying, 'I repent,'** you shall **forgive him.**"*

Luke 17:3-4

Somebody does the same thing to you seven times in one day, but each time they come to you and say, "I'm truly sorry. I repent." Jesus says you're to forgive. That may seem foolish or absurd. But haven't you come to God seven times (*or more*) in a day and asked *Him* to forgive *you*?

Yet how can you forgive someone if there's no remorse, no repentant spirit? There is a way. What you can do is take forgiveness from your heart and put it in the bank in escrow for them. Even if the individual can't accept it right now, you've given it. It is there. All they need to do is write the check of repentance and faith and they can receive that forgiveness.

Isn't that what Jesus did for us when He died on the cross? He provided forgiveness for us. It is there. But it is obtained only when we repent and receive it by faith. Once we do, we can pull from the abundance we've been given to make forgiveness available for that person to pick up, if they will. And even if they don't repent, you'll have laid it all down. You will have emptied it from your heart so you won't have to carry any kind of baggage or bitterness around with you.

When you truly forgive, you are freed from the bondage of bitterness. And there's no reason whatsoever you should be dragging around the chains of either bitterness or guilt. None of us is perfect. We fail each day in many ways, but we can still give God glory. There should not be one person on earth you have resentment toward. And you can make certain there's no hidden sin in your heart and life. That's not living on some elevated level of spirituality—it should be commonplace for any believer. That's simply the way we are to live and walk in faith: forgiven and free by the grace of God. What fools we are to drag these chains with us when we can start every day as clean and pure as the driven snow! (Psa. 51:7)

Did God convict you of something specific or are you being prompted to "open an account" of forgiveness? How will you respond in obedience?

_____
_____
_____
_____
_____
_____

What steps can you take to avoid draping your heart in the chains of guilt or bitterness and/or help others do the same?

_____
_____
_____
_____
_____
_____

If someone comes to mind for whom you need to put forgiveness in escrow, write out some specific prayers for that person today and begin earnestly lifting them to the Lord. Or find how you might encourage someone else to this action.

_____
_____
_____
_____
_____
_____

Help me not to misdirect my faith Lord, but to stay focused on You!

> *For the Scripture says, "Whoever believes **on Him** will not be put to shame."*
>
> Romans 10:11

True faith is measured by its object. Some well-meaning person may try to encourage you with words like these: "Just believe. Have faith!" But that begs these questions: *Faith in what? Believe whom?* The Bible never teaches us to have faith in faith. There's nothing magical or mystical about just believing. The power of faith is in its *object*. Our faith must rest in Almighty God if we do not want to be disappointed.

People also like to say, "Faith moves mountains." But that is not true. It is **God** that moves mountains. Jesus clarified this when talking to His disciples about faith that could move a mountain or wither a fig tree. He said: "Have faith in **God**" (Mark 11:22). The emphasis here is on **God**—for He alone is the source of mountain-moving power!

Faith in faith is mere positive thinking; it's mainly having faith in yourself. If you go that route, you're headed for a calamitous fall. Inevitably you'll come to a time of discouragement as you wonder, "How do I know my faith is good enough? Is my faith strong enough?" It's not primarily the strength of your faith that matters; it is the object of your faith. Never put faith in faith. Put faith in God.

The way to strengthen your faith is to get to know the Lord. Let God's Holy Spirit speak to you as you study His Word, which says: "Those who know Your name will put their trust in You" (Psa. 9:10). A great way to learn about God's character, His attributes and abilities is to study the names of God in Scripture. Daniel 11:32 says, "The people who know their God shall be strong, and carry out great exploits." God Himself is the object of faith; if you would have strong faith, you must get to know God. Because to know God is to love Him, and to love Him is to trust Him. To trust Him is to obey Him. And to obey Him is to be blessed—and never to be disappointed in Him!

What new thoughts did you find about getting to know God and increasing your faith? Some names of God you can reflect upon today: Adonai (Gen. 2:4); Jehovah Jireh (Gen. 22:14); Alpha and Omega (Rev. 21:6).

_____
_____
_____
_____
_____
_____

Did you ever experience a time of discouragement when you wondered if your faith was strong enough to sustain you? What could you do to continually examine your heart and make sure you aren't misdirecting your faith?

_____
_____
_____
_____
_____
_____

How could you help someone else understand the difference between positive thinking and truly having God as the object of their faith?

_____
_____
_____
_____
_____
_____

Give me a deeper desire to share my faith and bring souls to You, Lord.

*Then Peter...said: "...The word which God sent to the children of Israel, preaching peace through **Jesus Christ**—He **is Lord** of all...And we are witnesses of all things which He did...And **He commanded us** to preach to the people, and **to testify** that...**whoever believes in Him will receive remission of sins**."*

ACTS 10:34-43

Imagine this scenario: a man who is not a Christian—and, in fact, is of a different nationality and not familiar with your church or even your denomination—is inquiring about faith. So he invites you to come to his house where his family and friends are gathered, waiting for you to tell them why you believe in Jesus Christ. Would you be able to do that? Do you know what you'd say, how you might go about it?

This is what happened to the apostle Peter when a Gentile named Cornelius sent for him. And there's much we can learn from their God-ordained encounter. But the first thing to examine is not just your *readiness* to share your faith but your **willingness** to do so. It's one of the ways you know what you have is real: not only should you want to keep the faith—you should want to give it away! The best news this world has ever known is the saving Gospel of Jesus Christ. And you should have a desire to tell others about your wonderful Savior.

Did you know that to win souls is not only a command of God but a great privilege? One we are specifically given? Cornelius had been seeking God, and in response God sent an angel with a message. The angel told him to send for Simon Peter who would come and tell him and his household how to be saved. Why didn't the angel just share the Gospel instead of involving Peter? God never gave the Great Commission to angels; He gave it to human beings. (Mat. 28:19-20) We have a privilege that angels do not have. God never sent an angel to be a soul-winner; God has sent you. And when the opportunity arises, you should be ready to joyfully and confidently share your faith!

Take time to reacquaint yourself with the Great Commission. How are you endeavoring to respond to God's command to share your faith?

___

What keeps you from sharing your faith? Where do you find it most difficult to speak openly about Jesus and what He has done in your life? Consider how you could overcome this.

___

How could you help someone else to recognize this privilege and unique duty that is also theirs? Consider asking someone to hold you accountable to readily obey this command and look for opportunities to share Christ.

___

I praise You Jesus, that You are my risen Savior and Lord of all!

Then Peter...said: "...**Jesus Christ**—He is Lord of all...And **we are witnesses** of all things which He did...And **He commanded** us to preach to the people, and **to testify** that...**whoever believes in Him will receive remission of sins**."

Acts 10:34-43

Simon Peter, under direct divine orders and also by special invitation, went to the house of Cornelius, a Roman army officer, to share his faith. Until this time no Jew would enter a Gentile house like this to share spiritual things. But God had worked on Peter to convince him that He loves *all* people (Acts 11:4-18) and is not willing that *any* should perish. (2 Ptr. 3:9)

The door to salvation is wide but the path is narrow. All who are saved will be saved through faith in Jesus Christ or not at all. Cornelius was a devout man who gave generously to the poor and prayed to God regularly. But he needed to know that you come to God the Father only through Jesus Christ the Son. (John 14:6)

The people gathered at Cornelius' house that day were hungry to know God. Peter was able to present specific evidence that convicted and convinced them that Jesus is Lord of all. And God will help you use these same three proofs to bring others to Him: the personal confidence of the soul-winner, the powerful confirmation of the Scripture and the persuasive conviction of the Spirit.

When Peter shared his faith, it was with unwavering confidence. He had a rock-ribbed assurance—as did all of the other apostles. Though different from each other in many ways, these eleven men were unanimous about the fact that Jesus Christ is Lord. They all had the same confidence about Jesus' virtuous life, His vicarious death and His victorious resurrection. (Acts 10:37-40) They were eye-witnesses of these things, so sure of their faith that they would die for it; Peter eventually did. These believers could say beyond a shadow of a doubt, *"Jesus is alive! He is Lord of all!"* What a bold witness when **you** can say, "I know that I know these things are true. We serve a risen Savior!" It's this kind of personal confidence you'll need to be a soul-winner.

What's the difference between being *devout* and showing respect for God—and being *devoted to Christ* and willing to die for your faith?

___

Do you have a personal confidence concerning the life, death, burial and resurrection of Jesus? If asked to be a witness, what would you say?

___

Consider the lesson Peter learned through the vision God gave him in Acts 10. Is there anyone you might hesitate to share the Gospel with? Ask God to reveal any prejudices you may have and replace them with His love.

___

Open my heart, Lord, to hear the truth You have for me today.

*"...To Him **all the prophets** witness that, through His name, **whoever believes in Him** will receive remission of sins." While Peter was still speaking these words, **the Holy Spirit fell upon all those who heard** the word.*

Acts 10:42-44

Being an eyewitness of something isn't always enough. Someone may say you misinterpreted what you saw, made it up or even imagined it! So God gives us more than just personal confidence to help us share our faith. He gives a powerful confirmation through Holy Scripture. Peter told Cornelius and his household that *all* of the prophets give witness to Jesus. Over 300 Old Testament prophecies were directly fulfilled by Jesus. Do you know enough Scripture to open a Bible and convince someone about the Lord?

Even if you're not sure of your ability to navigate through Scripture, you just need to be obedient to share what you do know of Jesus. Speak your heart and be sincere. You don't want to be a salesperson when it comes to the Gospel, arguing someone into signing on the dotted line. You have to rely on God's Spirit to convict through the things you are sharing. And He will, because that's the third proof God gives to help in soul-winning—the persuasive conviction of the Holy Spirit. As Peter was sharing the truth he was confident of and showing how it was backed up by Scripture, the Spirit of God came upon all those who were hearing, believing and being gloriously saved!

Holy Spirit conviction is when the Spirit of God speaks to you and says, "That's true." He affirms in your heart that Jesus is the Son of God, that the Scriptures are true, and that the testimony of others is sincere. The Spirit can bear witness *in* your heart and also witness *through* you. (Acts 5:32) God didn't tell us that we have to go out and witness in our own strength. He gives us the Holy Spirit as an ally. (Acts 1:8) And if you are living in obedience, willing and ready to share your faith, the Spirit of God will direct you to opportunities, empower you to speak, and He will bring conviction through your life!

TAPESTRY

What blessings do you find in seeing how God makes provision for us to obey His command to be soul-winners?

___

Consider how all three proofs mentioned in the devotion can empower you to share your faith.

___

What Bible verses come to mind when you think of sharing Jesus with someone? How are you consistently hiding His Word in your heart that you might be ready to share the truth about Him?

___

Help me to always see baptism as an opportunity to reflect upon Your blessings and promises, Lord.

---

*Then Peter answered, "Can anyone forbid **water**, that these should not be **baptized** who have **received the Holy Spirit** just as we have?" And he commanded them to **be baptized in the name of the Lord**...*
                                                                ACTS 10:46-48

In a worship service, there may be an invitation and opportunity for people to come forward and declare their faith in Jesus Christ. And that is a very wonderful thing. But in the Bible, the real profession of faith is baptism. That's how a person said, "I am not ashamed of the Lord Jesus Christ" and became a part of the New Testament church. Baptism is the outward expression of an inward reality. One of the proofs that a person has truly put their trust in Christ is when they are willing to obey the Lord by taking that first step of believer's baptism.

This initial confession of faith is not incidental or accidental; it is fundamental. It's so important that Jesus commenced His public ministry by being baptized Himself—*not* because He was a sinner needing to show He had been saved; but to show that He would *become* the sin-bearer. Jesus identified Himself with sinful humanity through His baptism. We are baptized to identify ourselves with our saving Lord. Jesus also concluded His public ministry by commanding baptism. (Mat. 28:19) With all the things He could have said, Jesus chose to include baptism within His brief parting words. That's how vital it is. And we should never minimize what God has so maximized!

Baptism is that one symbolic act which preaches the Gospel over and over again. Each time a new believer is immersed beneath baptismal waters and then raised up again, we see the death, burial, and resurrection of Jesus Christ. How the devil would love to steal that message out of our churches! While baptism is not necessary for salvation, it is necessary for obedience. And obedience is necessary for fruitfulness, joy and growth in the Christian life.

Did you realize baptism is a *command*? Have a look at some other instances where baptism is mention in the Book of Acts: 2:41, 8:36-38, 9:17, 16:33. Consider why God chose to so emphasize this symbolic act of faith.

___

Our faith will only grow as we obey what God has already shown us to do. Were you baptized as an act of obedience *after* you came to Christ in repentance and faith? What other steps of obedience is He calling you to take today?

___

How could you use these truths to help someone else step out in faith and obey what God is commanding them to do?

___

Faith & Forgiveness

Let my life radiate with a visible, vibrant faith in You, dear Lord!

———

*Then they came to Him, bringing a paralytic who was **carried by four men**. And when they could not come near Him because of the crowd, they uncovered the roof where He was. So when they had broken through, they let down the bed on which the paralytic was lying. **When Jesus saw their faith**, He said to the paralytic, "Son, your **sins are forgiven** you."*

Mark 2:3-5

Real faith is the kind of faith you can see. (Jam. 2:18) Jesus Himself saw the faith of these men who brought their disabled friend to Him. It was no small task they undertook, and their visible, vibrant faith made it possible not just for this man to be healed physically—but more importantly to be saved spiritually!

We don't know their names, but we can just imagine one of these men was called "Mr. Compassion" because he cared for the paralyzed man. He had a heart like the Lord Jesus, Who saw the multitudes and was moved with compassion. (Mat. 9:36) Does it burden your heart to know that multitudes will die and go to hell if we don't tell them about Jesus?

Another man was "Mr. Confidence," who saw through eyes of faith what could be accomplished by God's grace. And "Mr. Courage" was there, for this was a courageous thing they did—going up on a rooftop, tearing up someone's property, barging into a crowded home. These men were willing to be a spectacle, to be ridiculed and to bear the costs of putting their faith into action. Some Christians are ashamed to carry a Bible to work or pray over a meal in public, mortified they might be seen as "fanatical" about their faith.

On the fourth corner was "Mr. Creativity," who came up with this rather ingenious way to get their friend to Jesus. Love will find a way. And this is what is so needed today—for people of compassion, confidence, courage and creativity to respond in faith and obedience to our Lord's command to "Go" (Mat. 28:19) and to lovingly bring all men, by all means, to Jesus Christ at any cost.

Read the rest of the story, Mark 2:6-12. What lessons do you find about our faith, God's forgiveness and physical healing?

___

Determine how much of each of these qualities you possess and consider how you could use that to reach others for Christ: compassion, confidence, courage and creativity.

___

These men most likely paid for the repairs of the roof they had damaged. When's the last time it **cost** you anything to help bring someone to Christ?

___

Faith & Forgiveness

Lord, show me what I can do to get my family into Your ark of safety.

---

*By faith Noah, being divinely warned of things not yet seen, moved with godly fear, **prepared an ark for the saving of his household...***

HEBREWS 11:7

Because Noah obeyed God and made preparation for his family to be spared, they were all safely together in the ark when God's wrath was being poured out upon the world.

The Bible teaches household faith—from Rahab to Cornelius there are many examples. (Jos. 2, Acts 10) Consider all that happened after the Philippian jailer asked Paul and Silas what he needed to do to be saved:

> So they said, "Believe on the Lord Jesus Christ, and you will be saved, you and your household." Then they spoke the word of the Lord to him and to all who were in his house....And immediately he and all his family were baptized...and he rejoiced, having believed in God with all his household. (Acts 16:31-34)

Now we should want everybody to come to faith in Jesus Christ. But don't you especially want your family to be saved and know the love of Jesus? Don't you want to know that all of you will one day be in heaven together?

Having a household faith doesn't mean you can believe in Christ on behalf of your children or family members and thus secure their salvation. But it certainly means you need to have some foresight; you need to make some preparation.

You can talk to your children and loved ones about the Lord carefully and prayerfully. Look for unique ways and opportunities to show His love to them. And if possible, sit down and speak face to face, heart to heart with them about your faith in Jesus. Pray continually that they might come to know Him as Savior. You need to say, "Lord, I want **all** my family to be aboard the ark of safety."

You can't begin to build when the rain starts falling; you have to make preparations for your household now, before it's too late. Noah prepared as God instructed—and He got his family into the ark.

Think of some things that are distinctive about your family and see how those things could play into the lessons God is showing you about household faith.

_____
_____
_____
_____
_____

The ark is a picture of the Lord Jesus Christ. How does your family see that you are resting securely in Jesus?

_____
_____
_____
_____
_____

Write the names of family members and loved ones you want to come aboard God's ark of safety. Pray for each of them specifically, earnestly and often. Ask God to bring opportunities for you to share your faith with them.

_____
_____
_____
_____
_____

Thank You for all that I inherit through You, Jesus!

By faith Noah, being divinely warned of things not yet seen, moved with godly fear, **prepared an ark** for the saving of his household, **by which he condemned the world and became heir** of the **righteousness** which is **according to faith**.

Hebrews 11:7

Noah condemned the world with a weather forecast. He told the people of his day about the flood, but they wouldn't believe him. He warned them of the coming judgment, but they refused to hear. In so doing they were condemned. They couldn't stand before God with the excuse that they didn't know. They just chose not to listen and thereby sealed their own fate. By *faith* and obedience, Noah and his family became the sole heirs of planet earth!

Have you ever thought about the vast amount of time, money and effort Noah put into that ark? Think of all the materials and labor required for what was perhaps a 120-year building project! And that ark was all he had to show for his life's work. The rest of the people of his day were buying and selling, marrying and giving in marriage (Mat. 24:38)—living high, wide and handsome, building their lives and their futures. They probably thought Noah was a fool to invest everything he had in the ark. But there came a dreadful turning point when all of their so-called real estate wasn't very real because it was under water; their bankroll couldn't even buy a raft for them to float on. They couldn't save their possessions, their children or themselves. They lost it all—while Noah gained it all.

When he stepped off that boat, the whole world was before him. He owned it all! But that's just a pittance compared to the real fortune he received. Noah became an *heir of righteousness*. His sins were forgiven; God gave him a new heart! He wasn't just saved from a flood; he was saved for all eternity. One day we'll meet Noah in heaven. He didn't *earn* righteousness; he **inherited it by faith**. The only way you can be made righteous is by trusting the Lord. That ark was a picture of Jesus. And Noah's faith has been for all time a picture of faith in the Lord Jesus Christ.

What new thoughts can you take from this lesson as you reflect on Noah's faith, his obedience and his inheritance?

_____
_____
_____
_____
_____

Consider where you're investing the majority of your time, money and efforts. What do you think you'll have to show for your life's work? Who will benefit from it and how?

_____
_____
_____
_____
_____
_____

What insights did you gain today that could help you reach out to others with God's truth?

_____
_____
_____
_____
_____
_____

Faith & Forgiveness

Lord, give me a persistent faith; may I not relent in pursuing You.

---

*...a woman of Canaan...cried out to Him, saying, "Have mercy on me, O Lord, Son of David! My daughter is severely demon-possessed." **But He answered her not a word**....Then she came and worshiped Him, saying, "Lord, help me!" But He answered..."It is not good to take **the children's bread** and throw it to the **little dogs**." And she said, "Yes, Lord, yet **even the little dogs eat the crumbs** which fall from their masters' table." Then Jesus answered..."O woman, **great is your faith**!"*

MATTHEW 15:22-28

Can you imagine Jesus treating anyone this way, let alone a heartbroken mother desperately seeking help for her child? There are many instances in the Bible where our Lord makes it *seem* as if He doesn't care, as if He doesn't want to hear or to bless. But He's really just testing, giving opportunity for someone to exercise their faith and push through to the blessings He has for them.

Jesus first appears to ignore this Canaanite woman. But she persists to the point of embarrassing the disciples. (v. 23) Even when He puts the truth to her so plainly that it sounds insulting, she is undeterred. How did she know to keep asking, keep seeking, keep knocking? (Mat. 7:7-8) She was a pagan, but she knew enough about Jesus to seek Him out. And she believed deeply enough that He could and would help her so as not to care what others thought of her...and not to let up until she had fully pleaded her case.

Most of us would likely just bow out if Jesus responded to us this way. But this woman knew exactly who and what she was, and she agreed with Jesus that she had no right to expect Israel's Messiah to help her before caring for those to whom He'd been sent. Yet she rightly recognized that there was enough grace to go around—even for "strays" like her. Her humility showed that she was relying solely on Jesus' mercy to grant her petition and bring healing to her daughter. This mother withstood the testing and pressed through in faith until she received what she so greatly desired: "And her daughter was healed from that very hour" (v. 28).

What blessings do you see here that encourage your faith? What new thoughts did you encounter about how our Lord may test our faith?

___
___
___
___
___
___

Read Matthew 7:7-8 to see how this Syrophoenician woman embodied the truth found there. And ask God to show you areas in your life where you need to be more persistent.

___
___
___
___
___
___

How could you help someone to be persistent in their faith and encourage them to push through to the blessings God has for them?

___
___
___
___
___
___

Faith & Forgiveness

Align my heart with Yours, Lord, as I take in Your Word today.

Now **Deborah**, a prophetess...called for **Barak**...and said to him, "Has not **the Lord God of Israel commanded**, 'Go and deploy troops at Mount Tabor; take with you ten thousand men...and against you I will deploy Sisera, the commander of Jabin's army...and I will deliver him into your hand'?" And Barak said to her, "**If you will go with me, then I will go**; but if you will not go with me, I will not go!"

Judges 4:4, 6-8

When God's message came to Barak through the prophetess Deborah, the response was not quite what you'd expect from a confident military leader. He agreed to go toward victory, but only if she went with him! Even though this man had a weak and fearful faith, he's still listed among the heroes of faith. (Heb. 11:32) It is not *great faith* in God we need nearly so much as faith *in a great God*.

Barak used what little faith he had. He planted that mustard seed and his faith continued to grow. We would do well to follow his example in two important areas. First, he heard and responded to the Word of God. Secondly, he associated himself with the people of God. Faith is as much caught as it is taught. And it was the faith of Deborah that encouraged the faith of Barak.

If you want your faith to grow, get with God's people and get in God's Word. It really is *that* simple. We are to exhort one another when we come to church. (Heb. 10:24-26) You can be part of a worship service where you hear the Bible being preached, join with other believers in praising God, and come away with a heart full of faith! Faith is nurtured as we come together and encourage each other in the Body of Christ.

Spend time with people of faith and before long you will have it, because faith is contagious. Remember, the infallible source of Barak's faith was the Word of God. You must know and love the Bible; saturate your soul with this Holy Book if you want faith. And align yourself with likeminded believers so your love and understanding of God's Word will grow reciprocally, along with your faith!

Barak was reluctant to go as God commanded. See how his victory was tarnished by his hesitancy (Jdg. 4:9, 17-21) and consider where God desires your eager obedience today.

_____
_____
_____
_____
_____
_____

Can you think of times when someone in your church has strongly urged you to do something, advised or even admonished you? This is what it means to exhort. How are you interacting with other believers in this faith-building way?

_____
_____
_____
_____
_____
_____

Could someone you know stand to be "strongly encouraged" by the truths you've encountered here today? What will you share with them and how?

_____
_____
_____
_____
_____
_____

Help me to be wise enough to join You in the direction You're going.

Then Deborah said to Barak, "Up! For **this is the day in which the Lord has delivered Sisera into your hand**. Has not the Lord gone out before you?" So Barak went down from Mount Tabor... **And the Lord routed Sisera** and all his chariots and all his army...**before Barak**...

Judges 4:14-15

One of the greatest military victories ever won was by this man named Barak, as he fought the good fight of faith. No doubt his foe, Sisera, was supremely confident as he rode into battle with superior forces, more experience and better weaponry—including 900 chariots of iron. (v. 3) But just as the two armies met, it began to rain...mightily.

This was truly an instance when "the bottom fell out," as described in Deborah's victory song: "The earth trembled and the heavens poured, the clouds also poured water; the mountains gushed before the Lord..." (Jdg. 5:4-5). The battlefield became a swamp, chariots bogged down in the mud, horses floundered. Recounting the battle, Josephus, a secular historian, spoke of a violent storm with heavy winds that drove rain and hail against the faces of the Canaanites, rendering most of their weaponry useless. But he noted that the storm was behind the Israelites causing them less harm and giving them the impetus to drive into the middle of their disarrayed enemy and defeat them. God gave a marvelous victory that day because of a rainstorm.

Now, we know the promise of Romans 8:28: "all things work together for good to those who love God...who are the called according to His purpose." But the other side of that is: *all things fight against the man who fights against God!*" They fought from the heavens; the stars from their courses fought against Sisera" (Jdg. 5:20). Sisera was defeated before he ever started. The whole universe was against this man! Wisdom in the simplest form is just to find out what direction God is going and to join Him. If you don't, you're headed for a collision with the stars. Sin can't win! Faith can't fail! Barak had a weak faith, but it was a weak faith in a great God. And because of that, the whole universe was behind him.

What blessings do you find in seeing how God aligned all of nature behind His man, Barak, who was acting in obedience to God's call?

_____
_____
_____
_____
_____
_____

We encounter battles in our own lives each day. Read Psalm 20:6-8 for more on where to place your trust when facing adversity.

_____
_____
_____
_____
_____
_____

What truths from this lesson could you share with a friend or loved one to help bolster their faith in the midst of what they're battling?

_____
_____
_____
_____
_____
_____

Help me to trust You Lord, even when things don't go as I expect.

---

*And He said to them, "What kind of conversation is this that you have with one another **as you walk and are sad?**"...So they said to Him, "The things concerning Jesus of Nazareth...our rulers delivered Him to be condemned to death, and crucified Him. **But we were hoping that it was He who was going to redeem Israel.**"*

Luke 24:17-21

Two dismal disciples trudged along a country road, sad and disillusioned. Just three days prior they'd seen Jesus crucified and buried. Now they'd heard stories of His resurrection, but they didn't know for certain He was alive. They were half-believing, half-doubting. Unable to see past their own disappointment, they let their doubt lead them to discouragement and then to despondency.

This was all rooted in misunderstanding and unbelief. They were looking for a political Messiah to throw off the yoke of Rome and redeem Israel. Their hopes were set on a kingdom which they'd heard about from the prophets, the poets and even Jesus. They thought they'd found their king. But then He was crucified. And His kingdom shrank to the narrow confines of a rock-hewn tomb. These disciples were confused and distraught because they couldn't see the whole picture. But it was their ignorance of God's Word that kept them from understanding. (v. 25)

Had they believed all the truth they'd been shown, they would have known there was more. Jesus wasn't finished when they laid His body in that tomb. He was doing exactly what He came to do: conquering sin and death and reclaiming what man had lost to Satan. (1 Cor. 15:55) And now the resurrected Savior was about to ascend to heaven and send His Holy Spirit to endow the disciples with incredible power so they could have a blessed part in ushering in the Kingdom of heaven! And *that* was the miraculous, glorious "big picture" they were missing out on due to their lack of understanding...which stemmed from a lack of faith.

TAPESTRY

Instead of rejoicing in Jesus' resurrection, these men were missing out on some of the most marvelous blessings faith affords! What does this say to you about the things that can block our vision for God's plans and purposes?

_____
_____
_____
_____
_____
_____

Have you ever been disappointed with God when something didn't turn out as you hoped or expected? How did this affect your faith? Are you able to trust Him even when you can only see part of the story?

_____
_____
_____
_____
_____
_____

What can you share with someone whose hopes have been dashed to help them see the bigger picture that God has something more in store for them?

_____
_____
_____
_____
_____
_____

Thank You, Lord, that You continue to show us marvelous things about Yourself in all the Scriptures.

Then He said to them, **"O foolish ones, and slow of heart to believe in all that the prophets have spoken!** Ought not the Christ to have suffered these things and to enter into His glory?" And beginning at Moses and all the Prophets, He expounded to them **in all the Scriptures** the things concerning **Himself.**

Luke 24:25-27

Notice what Jesus says about a person who doesn't believe all of the Bible. You can't foolishly pick and choose what parts of God's Word you want to accept, or you'll end up as troubled and confused as these disciples were. Yet Jesus came alongside them in their disheartened state and provided what they were lacking.

The blessing here is that—even though they were filled with doubt and Jesus had to call them foolish—these men did sincerely love the Lord. They had just lost the joy of their salvation. And Jesus sought them. He drew near to them and walked with them. (v. 15) He went after these doubting disciples not to condemn them, but to comfort and restore them. When the Lord Jesus Christ saves you, the love of God is like a strong rubber band. He puts it around you, and you may stray off, but He just keeps drawing you back to Himself. He just keeps seeking you. We were saved because He sought us. And if He would seek us when we were His enemies, how much more will He seek us now that we are His own dear children? (Rom. 5:10)

These disciples were just struggling in their faith due to what they had not believed or understood of God's Word. So Jesus taught them. He gave a 7-mile Bible conference on that Emmaus Road. Beginning in Genesis, He showed how His ancestry, birth, infancy, manhood, career, teaching, preaching, reception, rejection, suffering, death, burial, resurrection, ascension and Second Coming were all written of in a marvelous way...centuries before He was born. And their hearts began to burn within them as the flame of faith was rekindled.

Think of our resurrected Lord listening in on and then joining in the conversation with these two sad men, knowing their faith was about to be joyfully restored! What particular blessings do you find in this lesson?

_____
_____
_____
_____
_____
_____

What is it that you struggle with or would like to know more about in God's Word? Ask Him to give you understanding as you earnestly delve into the Scriptures.

_____
_____
_____
_____
_____
_____

What truths stand out in this lesson as something you might share to encourage someone else's faith?

_____
_____
_____
_____
_____
_____

Open my heart to Your truth that I may see You with spiritual eyes.

Then their eyes were opened and they knew Him; and He vanished from their sight. And they said to one another, "Did not our **heart burn within us** while He talked with us on the road, and **while He opened the Scriptures to us?**"

Luke 24:31-32

The risen Lord had walked with them, talked with them, taught them and ministered to them. Yet these disciples had not recognized it was Jesus Who was with them all the while on the road to Emmaus. Even though He was in a resurrected body, they didn't know it was Him. Their eyes had been restrained. (v. 16)

When these men were plodding along, struggling to decide what they believed about Jesus' death and resurrection, He could have just said, "Look, here I am! Believe!" But He wanted to grow their faith in a vital new way that would help prepare them for what was about to happen. Jesus was getting ready to go to Heaven and He didn't want the disciples to rely upon knowing Him by His physical presence. He wanted them to know Him because of His spiritual reality through the Scriptures. He didn't allow them to recognize Him using their physical eyesight, so that they might learn to use their spiritual vision.

It's significant that it was the Word and not the physical sense which made Jesus real to them. They didn't say, "Oh yes, that was really Him! We saw Him with our own eyes." Instead they said, "We knew Him because He opened the Word to us." As their hearts began to resonate with the truth He was revealing, they came to know Him in the same way we do today. Jesus Christ is made real to us through the written Word illumined by His Spirit.

These men enjoyed intimate, individual, uninterrupted fellowship with Jesus as they walked with Him for miles. He was preparing them to walk in the same way after He was gone—assured of His presence with them, receiving His words of wisdom, feeling their hearts respond to His. They could continue with all of this— walking now by faith, not merely by sight. (2 Cor. 5:7)

Consider the intimate interaction these disciples enjoyed with the risen Lord. Think of having the same sweet fellowship with Jesus as you walk with Him by faith. How does this bless you?

_____
_____
_____
_____
_____
_____

When you read God's Word, is Jesus real to you? Do you hear His Holy Spirit speaking to you and feel your heart responding to His truth? Ask God to sharpen your spiritual vision and show you more of Himself today.

_____
_____
_____
_____
_____
_____

What truths did you find here that will allow you to share with someone else how Jesus Christ can be real to them?

_____
_____
_____
_____
_____
_____

Lord, how could I not be excited that You are alive in me? Let me live with a holy enthusiasm that makes people take notice!

*And they said…"Did not our **heart burn within us** while He talked with us on the road, and while He opened the Scriptures to us?" So they rose up **that very hour** and returned to Jerusalem…saying, "**The Lord is risen indeed**…"*

Luke 24:32-34

No longer doubting. No longer despondent. No longer discouraged. These disciples were so excited they had to get back to their friends right away to let them know the wonderful news: *It's true*—Jesus really is alive!

Now that's something we should get excited about too! But so much of our worship today is characterized by dead orthodoxy…when what we need is a living faith. We need burning hearts that are set on fire from heaven! On the Day of Pentecost, the mark of the Holy Spirit was a cloven tongue of fire. (Acts 2:3) In fact, the disciples were so moved by the Spirit that day that they were accused of being drunk. When's the last time anyone accused you of being drunk over your faith? Why is it that we cannot have that holy, reckless, heartfelt abandon that the early church had?

These men—whose hearts went from burdened to believing to burning within them—could not contain their excitement and immediately hurried back to Jerusalem with the good news. You might as well tell the sun not to shine as to tell these people not to witness about a risen Savior. Now, we believe Jesus is risen. But how has that really affected our faith? We need to be able to say with irrepressible enthusiasm that He is *definitely, certainly, truly without a doubt* risen, that He's alive and well today—and living in us! May the things we believe *take hold of us*, that we too would have a heartfelt religion fueled by a blazing, passionate, emotional love for the Lord Jesus Christ—Who is risen, *indeed*!

When is the last time you were irrepressibly enthusiastic about your faith? What is God impressing upon your heart to do in response to this lesson?

___

How can you kindle and keep a passionate, genuine, emotional love for the Lord Jesus that won't be diminished by life's daily grind?

___

When you want to share the good news of the Gospel, how much more effective would your message be if people could truly see an enthusiasm for the things of Christ bubbling over in your life?

___

Cleanse my heart, Lord, and prepare it to receive the truth You have for me today.

***By faith** Abel offered unto God **a more excellent sacrifice than Cain**...*
Hebrews 11:4

The world's first martyr heads the list of those recognized for their faith in Hebrews chapter 11. Abel demonstrates to us the definite difference that faith makes in religion. (Gen. 4:4-5)

It's not true that all religions are equal. Today we're expected to put our arms around everyone and embrace their belief system or we're bigoted. And new forms of "spirituality" are popping up every day. But no matter the categories or denominations, there are really only two kinds of religion in the world: the true and the false. False religion is salvation by works, relying on human effort and merit. True religion is salvation by grace through faith in the shed blood of the Lord Jesus Christ. Both are represented in Cain and Abel.

Cain was a farmer, a tiller of the ground, and God had said, "Cursed is the ground." (Gen. 3:17) Cain was also a sinner because he was a son of Adam and the Bible says, "In Adam all die." (1 Cor. 15:22) So you have a man with wicked hands bringing the fruit of the cursed ground as an offering to the Lord.

Now, it probably looked like a county fair as Cain laid out this plenteous array of beautiful fruits and vegetables, fragrant flowers and lush vegetation. He was being very religious, but it was a religion of his own ingenuity. Cain didn't get this idea by divine revelation. It was not rooted in the Word of God; therefore it didn't come by faith. So it was impossible to please God with this offering. (Heb. 11:6) Cain was displaying the results of his hard work and perspiration. And it takes a lot of sweat to be a farmer. But God wasn't looking for sweat. He had established that the shedding of blood was necessary for the forgiveness of sins. (Heb. 9:22) Cain brought vegetables. You can't get blood from a turnip. God rejected Cain's bloodless sacrifice and his religion of self-effort.

Do you ever find yourself falling into this trap of relying on your own self-efforts? What can you do to keep the tenets of Cain's false religion from creeping into your worship?

_____
_____
_____
_____
_____
_____

Have you been pressured to show acceptance for someone's beliefs when you know their religion is contrary to the Gospel of Christ? What could you do to show love to the person but still stand for truth?

_____
_____
_____
_____
_____
_____

What truths can you share with someone to help them turn from false religion to faith in Jesus Christ?

_____
_____
_____
_____
_____
_____

Thank You, Jesus, for Your perfect sacrifice made for me!

> ***By faith*** *Abel offered unto God **a more excellent sacrifice than Cain**, through which he obtained witness that **he was righteous**...and through it he being dead still speaks.*
>
> Hebrews 11:4

Abel, a shepherd, selected from the best of his flock and made an animal sacrifice to God, representing the shed blood of the Lord Jesus Christ. He did so in faith and obedience. How could Abel have faith to present a pleasing offering to the Lord unless God had first revealed what kind of sacrifice He wanted?

The first Gospel sermon had already been preached when Adam and Eve learned the consequences of their sin. God told how the Seed of the woman would bruise the head of the serpent—foretelling how Jesus will crush Satan's head! (Gen. 3:15) Then God gave an illustration when He shed innocent blood to clothe Adam and Eve in garments of animal skin. (3:21) They had tried to cover the shame of their nakedness with fig leaves they'd sewn together. But the works of their hands would not suffice. They hid from the presence of the Lord because the religion of man's works cannot stand the all-piercing gaze of a righteous, Holy God!

In Abel's offering, we see the shadow of the cross. The Bible says Abel was a prophet. (Luke 11:51) He lived at the dawn of human history as we know it, yet he brought a blood sacrifice, for God had revealed by precept and example the need for blood atonement. (Lev. 17:11)

Cain had the same opportunity to respond in obedience to God as Abel did. But he chose to follow his own desires rather than to do well in God's sight. (Gen. 4:7) Cain destroyed his own life and eternity with the fatal blows he dealt to his brother. Abel yet lives and still speaks of true faith. His story forever points to the blood that was shed...not merely his own, but the blood of the spotless Lamb Who was slain from the foundation of the world.

What blessings do you find in seeing God's loving care for His children—making garments to cover them after they'd disobeyed and sorely disappointed Him?

_____
_____
_____
_____
_____
_____

Look at the things you're offering to God [consider your tithe, your time, your worship]. What do they reveal about your heart?

_____
_____
_____
_____
_____
_____

What do you find here that could help you tell someone about God's spotless Lamb?

_____
_____
_____
_____
_____
_____

Cleanse my heart, Lord, that I might worship You today in Spirit and in truth.

---

*By faith **Abel offered unto God a more excellent sacrifice** than Cain...**and through it he being dead still speaks***.

HEBREWS 11:4

Of Adam and Eve's two sons, one was a murderer, the other a martyr. In Greek the word *martyr* and the word *witness* are the same word. Death doesn't make martyrs, it simply reveals them.

Both brothers presented the Lord an offering, but one worshipped in Spirit and truth, the other by his own ingenuity. Abel's offering showed his love for God; Cain's showed his love for himself. His contrived religion was based on culture, not Calvary. Perhaps Cain was too refined to offer a blood sacrifice. But he was not too refined to cause his brother's blood to flow so freely it cried out to God from the ground. (Gen. 4:10) Cain's heart was revealed in his errant, angry, and then deadly actions.

The first murder was over religion. And it was a religious crowd that crucified Jesus. False religion is almost always murderous, just like its founder, Satan himself. (John 8:44) Think of what is happening in the world today. All over the globe people are being murdered in the name of religion. We have many modern day martyrs—believers who are showing the love of the Lord Jesus Christ and paying with their blood. False religion is characterized by force. Our faith is characterized by love. And it is never, ever coerced.

For the child of God, death is not a period, but a comma. Abel lives on, as do all the others who came after him and also died for their faith. All have won the martyr's crown: "...which the Lord has promised to those who love Him" (Jam. 1:12). Abel has been in heaven for thousands of years, and ten million years from now he will still be praising the Lord along with all the saints and his righteous acts will still be giving a testimony of God's love and grace.

See what God said to Cain about temptation in Genesis 4:5-8; then read what is said about those who will receive the martyr's crown in James 1:12. What is God saying about loving Him and obeying Him?

_____
_____
_____
_____
_____
_____

Consider how you would feel about having someone else's views and beliefs forced upon you and how you might respond.

_____
_____
_____
_____
_____
_____

Are you connected to any missionaries serving the Lord in other countries? Consider how you could be praying for and supporting others who are spreading the faith abroad.

_____
_____
_____
_____
_____
_____

Lord, please illumine the paths You would have me to pursue.

*Now **this is the confidence that we have in Him**, that if we ask anything **according to His will**, He hears us. And if **we know that He hears us**, whatever we ask, **we know that we have** the petitions that we have asked of Him.*

1 John 5:14-15

When you set goals and objectives for your life, how do you know they're God-given and not just your daydreams? A daydream begins with you; a vision comes from God. When you believe your vision is from Him, only then can you exercise faith. Like the men and women of faith in Hebrews 11 who acted upon what they heard from God, you want to be: *saturated with Scripture, separated from sin, dedicated to the Savior, and activated by the Spirit.* But as you're purposing to do those things, you still need to know if the objectives you've put forth are God's will so you can have faith to pursue them.

God promises to fully illumine the way so you can be certain of the direction you're taking: "But the path of the just is like the shining sun, that shines ever brighter unto the perfect day" (Pro. 4:18) Notice this process isn't immediate, but gradual, like the sun rising in the sky. At first it's dark and you can't see a thing. Then it's gray dawn and you can see dimly, no color, just shapes. And then the sun comes up and you see color, but there are long shadows. Then as the sun rises to a perfect day, high noon, it's full of color and no shadows. That's the way it is when you're finding the will of God.

So when you want to know if something is God's will for you, bring it before Him and ask: "Is this Your will for me, Lord...in my business?...in my health?...in my finances?...with my children?...in my church?" Whatever it may be, just put it before Him. And as God begins to speak, you listen and say, "Lord, if this is You, just keep speaking." And the light will shine more and more unto a perfect day.

How are you encouraged by the promises of God to show you His clear direction for your life?

_____
_____
_____
_____
_____
_____

In what areas of your life do you need to set some God-given goals and begin to move toward them? Write out some specific objectives and begin to pray over those now.

_____
_____
_____
_____
_____
_____

What insights did you find that can help you share godly wisdom with someone else seeking direction in their life?

_____
_____
_____
_____
_____
_____

Thank You, Lord, for loving me and forgiving me freely.

And be kind to one another, tenderhearted, **forgiving** *one another, even as God in Christ* **forgave** *you.*

EPHESIANS 4:32

Giving and receiving *true forgiveness* is important—not merely accepting an apology or glossing over an offense. When a person comes to you for forgiveness, pride may cause you to respond, "Oh, that's alright. Don't worry about it. It doesn't matter." But it *does* matter. You were hurt; you just don't want them to *know* you've been hurt. You'd rather rise above it all, so you act like it was "no big deal." Is your relationship with that person a "big deal"? Then you want to treat their request with the importance it deserves. Acknowledge it and afford them the full forgiveness they seek.

You are to forgive fully. This doesn't mean just "forgetting about it." Do you think that's what God does when you come to Him for forgiveness? God "remembers our sins no more" only because they have been forgiven. (Heb. 8:12) Forgetting is never the means of forgiveness; it is the result. Neither of you can forget in the true sense of the word until the offense is removed. So don't be cavalier or casual; give earnest consideration to the person who asks for forgiveness and grant it so you can both put it behind you and move forward together in faith.

Likewise, if you're asking someone to forgive you, make certain it is forgiveness you get. Pride can get in the way here too. Many times we're too proud to admit we've done wrong. So you may go to a person and say, "**If** I've wronged you, I'm sorry." But that's not a confession. If you **know** you've done wrong, say so. And don't settle for a "Don't worry about it" response from them. Let them know you *are* worried about it; you're concerned for the relationship you share. You need to know they're truly willing to forgive what you fully acknowledge you've done—so healing can begin. (Jam. 5:16)

What lessons did you find here about giving and receiving the kind of forgiveness that brings healing?

_____
_____
_____
_____
_____

Is your faith hindered by any barrier of unforgiveness in your heart? Consider if you need to grant true forgiveness or seek it from anyone today.

_____
_____
_____
_____
_____

Do you know someone who needs to clear the way for healing in their life by seeking forgiveness from another? What truths might you lovingly share to help them do this?

_____
_____
_____
_____
_____

Lord, may I have faith to do the impossible today, if You bid me to!

...Jesus spoke to them, saying, "Be of good cheer! **It is I***; do not be afraid." And Peter...said, "Lord, if it is You, command me to come to You on the water." So* **He said, "Come***." And...***he walked on the water** *to go to Jesus. But when he saw that the wind was boisterous, he was afraid; and beginning to sink he cried out... "Lord, save me!" And immediately Jesus stretched out His hand and caught him, and said to him,* ***"O you of little faith, why did you doubt?"***

MATTHEW 14:27-31

Most of the terrified disciples thought they were seeing a ghost when Jesus appeared in the midst of the fierce storm—*walking* on the tumultuous sea! (v. 26) But Peter caught a glimpse of the great I AM. He saw Christ as totally victorious over the very thing threatening to engulf them. He wasn't thrill-seeking when he asked to come to Jesus on the water; he was asking to join in the victory. He was saying, "Lord, I want to put my feet where Your feet are and triumph over this storm too!" Jesus wants you to share in the victory with Him and realize that whatever is over your head is really under His feet. But you have to have a vision for that. You must see Jesus as the overcomer. (John 16:33)

And you have to hear Him. Peter didn't start out until he was ordered. Had he just jumped out of the boat, he would have sunk. That would have been presumption, not faith. And had Peter *not* stepped out after Jesus bid him to, it would have been disobedience and absolute unbelief. Faith is getting a word from God and acting on it. When you're listening for Jesus, He'll tell you what to do. You don't jump out of the boat until you hear God, but position yourself to see Him and hear Him and be ready to obey when He speaks to you.

God didn't tell all the disciples to get out of the boat, only Peter. But He had a plan for every one of them. And He has a plan for you. Faith isn't believing God can get you out of your problems. It's trusting the Lord and obeying when He calls you to get out of the boat and walk with Him in victory amid the storm.

Even though Peter had a "sinking spell," his faith still allowed him to experience victory on a miraculous level! And Jesus did not let him drown. What are some of the blessings you find in this?

_____
_____
_____
_____
_____
_____

Jesus has overcome the world and all things are under His feet. (Eph. 1:22) How does this give you strength for what you're facing today?

_____
_____
_____
_____
_____
_____

How can you use these truths to encourage someone else who's in the midst of a storm right now?

_____
_____
_____
_____
_____
_____

Help me not to withhold any of my heart from You, Lord.

...that Christ may **dwell** *in your hearts* **through faith**...

EPHESIANS 3:17

For the believers at Ephesus, Paul prayed not that they would ask Christ into their hearts—they already had—but that they would make Christ Sovereign. The word *dwell* implies permanent control by one who is the undisputed owner of a property. We're not just to give Jesus **a** place but to put Him in **first** place over all else in our lives.

The minute you establish His Lordship, several things will happen. First, you'll have a new realization of Christ's presence. He'll be a living, bright reality to you. Next, there'll be the reproduction of His purity. We're called to live a holy life like Jesus lived (1 Ptr. 1:15-16), but there's nothing in our flesh that will make us holy. If Jesus doesn't do it, it's not going to be done! That's why many of us are failing as we try to walk by faith. But when Jesus is given preeminence, the next result you'll find is the power of the resurrected Christ working through you!

The devil doesn't want you to enthrone Jesus and discover the authority you have in Him. The story is told of a wealthy man named Sir John Ramsden who wanted to control a little town in England. He'd been able to acquire every piece of property—save one, belonging to an old immoveable Quaker. Sir John himself went to the Quaker and generously offered to cover every inch of his property in gold sovereigns as a purchase price. The old Quaker said with a twinkle in his eye, "If you stand them all on edge sideways, we might talk." Since that was out of the question, a dejected Ramsden turned to leave. The Quaker said, "Remember, Sir John: Huddersfield belongs to thee and to me." Satan could be taunting Jesus the same way about you, saying, "Yes, that person belongs to You; but there's a part that still belongs to me." Is there a hell's half acre somewhere in your life that Satan inhabits, or have you enthroned the Lord Jesus Christ over all?

Make sure Christ **dwells** in your heart by faith as the supreme, undisputed head of your life. Write out a prayer to let Him know you want to take yourself off the throne and enthrone Him completely so His presence will be evident in your life.

_____
_____
_____
_____
_____
_____

You accepted Jesus Christ by faith; but how do you think you exercise faith daily to keep Him enthroned in your life?

_____
_____
_____
_____
_____
_____

Paul was praying for believers he loved to know the spiritual realities spoken of here. Who comes to your mind to pray for as Paul did?

_____
_____
_____
_____
_____
_____

I lay all that I have before You, Lord, with a grateful heart.

*He who is **faithful in what is least is faithful also in much**; and he who is unjust in what is least is unjust also in much. Therefore **if you have not been faithful** in the unrighteous mammon, who will **commit to your trust the true riches**?*

Luke 16:10-11

Sometimes people try to say wealth isn't a spiritual topic. But 16 of the 38 parables Jesus spoke dealt with man's relationship to material things and his use of money and possessions. For believers, this sensitive subject should be simple and straightforward. It comes down to faith: trusting God with all we have and being faithful stewards of what we've been given!

God instructs us to tithe—not because He needs or wants our money, but because we need to give it. It's an indication of our faith in the Lord. Giving a portion of your income back to Him (Pro. 3:9-10) acknowledges that it's God's money, not yours. Not just a tenth but *all* of it belongs to Him. The earth is the Lord's. You don't have one thing that God didn't give you. And you cannot help God out. He's already got it all. (Psa. 50:10-12)

Tithing is not something we do for God; it is something God does for us. It's your way to get blessed beyond measure! (Mal. 3:8-10) Someone asks, "Why should a little widow living on a pension tithe? God doesn't need that money." No, He doesn't. But she needs to see God moving in her life, fulfilling His promises. She needs to learn she can do more with nine-tenths and God as a partner than she can with ten-tenths by herself. It's a matter of faith. The tithe is symbolic of our complete reliance on the Lord.

The way you handle your finances shows how you would handle spiritual riches. You may be lacking spiritually because you've not been faithful with "your" money. And if God cannot trust you with **His** money, how can He trust you with greater, spiritual riches? You'll never have victory in your Christian life and know the blessings God wants you to have until you get honest with God about your finances—release everything to Him in faith!

Could you be more faithful in your tithe? Give more to missions? Where is God asking you to step out in faith in your finances?

_____
_____
_____
_____
_____
_____
_____

In Malachi 3:8-10 God actually challenges us to put Him to the test in what He promises to do. How could your faith grow if you take Him up on His challenge?

_____
_____
_____
_____
_____
_____
_____

The gist of the parable in Luke 16:1-8 is to use what God has given you to win souls to Christ. And one day in heaven you'll be greeted by many friends, grateful for your faithfulness! (v. 9) How are you investing in eternal treasures?

_____
_____
_____
_____
_____
_____
_____

May I live each day in humble gratitude for Your grace, dear Lord.

For the promise that he would be the heir of the world was not to Abraham...through the law, but through the righteousness of **faith**. *For if those who are of the law are heirs,* **faith** *is made void and the promise made of no effect...Therefore* **it is of faith** *that it might be* **according to grace**, *so that the* **promise might be sure to all**...

ROMANS 4:13-16

Paul, a great logician anointed by the Holy Spirit, makes a simple but substantial argument: salvation is by grace and, therefore, it *must* be of faith. Pointing to God's promise to Abraham, Paul explains that if there is *anything* required for salvation *other* than faith, it can't be God's gift of grace to all.

If salvation were given on the basis of merit or performance, some would inevitably be excluded. Suppose God said, "Everybody who wants to be saved, give $100." That may seem simple enough. But some people don't have $100. Suppose He said, "Everyone who wants to be saved, run around the block." Some with physical limitations could not comply. There is one thing that anyone and everyone can do: believe! You see, God makes it so simple. We have only to believe and receive with a repentant heart. If it took more than that to secure our salvation, it would not be of grace.

And you could not be certain of it. You could never be completely sure from one minute to the next that you are saved. Even if you had to rely on works for just one percent of your salvation—if *any* percentage was dependent upon you, you could never be sure! Someone might ask, "Are you saved?" You would have to reply along these lines: "Well, I hope so. I'm doing the best I can. I lived pretty well today—although I did lose my temper when that guy cut me off in traffic. I sure hope I'm saved!" But keeping your temper doesn't keep you saved. Thank God the security of your salvation doesn't depend on anything other than the action God has already taken. It can only be through God's grace; therefore it must be **by faith** that the promise is sure. And it is sure to **all**, because believing is something *everyone* can do!

What promises are you claiming today that give you unshakeable confidence in God's grace?

_____
_____
_____
_____
_____
_____

When we think of "<u>G</u>od's <u>R</u>iches <u>A</u>t <u>C</u>hrist's <u>E</u>xpense," we know we couldn't earn this grace because we could never repay Christ for His sacrifice! But how are you showing gratitude for His grace in your life each day?

_____
_____
_____
_____
_____
_____

Is there anyone you know who might be questioning their salvation? What could you share with them about God's gift of grace through faith alone?

_____
_____
_____
_____
_____
_____

May others see in my life the fruit of a living, vibrant faith!

---

*What does it profit...if someone **says** he has **faith** but does not have works? **Can faith save him?**...**faith** by itself, **if it does not have works, is dead.***

JAMES 2:14, 17

Paul said our salvation is by grace through faith alone. (Eph. 2:8-9) He was teaching about the *means* by which we receive salvation. There's no contradiction when James speaks here of works as the *proof* that salvation *has been* received. Paul spoke of the root of faith deep in a person's heart, which only God can see. But James is concerned with the fruit that should be evident if the root is truly there and thriving. It's not a "know so" but a "show so" salvation James puts forth by helping us examine the faith that shows **no signs of life**.

As we consider a **dead faith**, some appropriate epitaphs come to mind. The first is this: *Words without Works Are Worthless.* James questions the validity of a faith that does not change your life. The original Greek wording asks, "Can *that* faith save him?" Then he gives an illustration (vv. 15-16) which today would be akin to this: A friend comes to you destitute, in rags, needing food and clothes. You pat him on the back and send him on his way, saying: "Have a blessed day! Be well in the Lord! He's all you need!"—and you do nothing to meet his physical needs. *What good did your words do?* Just as empty words cannot clothe and feed a naked, hungry man, merely repeating hollow words cannot save and transform a life.

Rattling off a little prayer will not save you. Pious platitudes can't get you to heaven. And *saying* you believe does not mean you have true faith. What a person says is not necessarily fact. Abraham Lincoln is said to have asked a little boy, "If a dog has four legs and you call his tail a leg, how many legs does he have?" The answer is four. Because: "No matter what you call his tail, it's still a tail." No matter what a man claims about his faith, if it hasn't changed his life, it's just say-so. And we could write: *Words without Works Are Worthless* on the gravestone of his lifeless faith.

121 TAPESTRY

What lessons did you find here about believing what a person may say about their faith? What impact could these insights have on your spiritual life?

_____
_____
_____
_____
_____
_____

How do you think examining lifeless faith could challenge you in your personal walk each day?

_____
_____
_____
_____
_____
_____

Do you know anyone who "talks a good religion" but whose words ring hollow? Consider how you can approach them lovingly with God's truth.

_____
_____
_____
_____
_____
_____

Thank You, Lord, for the peace and assurance true faith brings.

———◆———

You believe that there is one God. You do well. *Even the demons believe—and tremble!* But do you want to know, O foolish man, that faith without works is dead?

JAMES 2:19-20

Did you know the Devil professes faith in God? He certainly believes God exists. And he knows more about Scripture than most Christians. In fact, he has more faith than some theological professors. Now, the Devil does not *possess* salvation—he will never willingly bow the knee to Jesus as Lord! But he believes in God, and he doesn't mind saying so.

Think of what Satan has openly confessed about Jesus. He admits Jesus is the Son of God. (Mat. 8:28-29) He acknowledges Jesus is the Holy One, pure and sinless. (Mark 1:23-24) He even declares Jesus is the Christ (Luke 4:41), the Messiah come to redeem the world. Satan would get an "A" in Systematic Theology in seminary. This tells us you can have profession without possession. You can know and openly agree with the facts of the Gospel without ever having laid hold of the grace that saves you. Making a profession of faith doesn't mean you're any more saved than the Devil is!

Satan is a real believer—so much so that it causes him to tremble. The word *tremble* here speaks of shuddering; it literally means "to stand up straight," like the hair stands up on the back of your neck when you're afraid. Real faith does not cause you to shudder. It brings peace. (Rom. 5:1)

Sadly, churches are filled with people who are just as orthodox as the Devil. They've gone through some theological exercise—walked an aisle, recited a creed, signed a card and had their picture added to the church directory. They think because of their "profession" they have possession. But they've never bowed the knee to Jesus Christ and accepted Him as their Lord and Savior. Tragically, they're going to miss heaven by some eighteen inches. They have the Gospel in their head but not in their heart. And we could put on the tombstone of their dead faith: *Profession without Possession Is Profitless.*

What rituals and rote religious activities might be steering you toward orthodoxy instead of a vibrant, thriving faith?

___

Look in Matthew 8:29 and Mark 1:24 and consider what more the demons alluded to knowing. Thank God the Devil is a defeated foe destined for destruction and his day of torment is coming!

___

Do you know anyone who seems to think of God in a sort of fearful, cringing way? How might you share with them that perfect love casts out fear? (1 John 4:18)

___

I praise You, Lord, for giving me life and filling me with Your Spirit.

*...Show me **your faith** without **your works**, and I will show you my faith **by my works**...For as the body without the spirit is dead, so faith without works is dead also.*

JAMES 2:18, 26

James gives us one more epitaph for a dead faith: *Form without Force Is Fatal.* What good is a body of truth without the life of the Spirit? As a Christian, you are animated by the life of God in you. A person without saving faith is still dead in their sin. That's why James says true faith is revealed by works, and he affirms this with two examples and one powerful illustration.

He shows how Abraham's faith was proved when he offered Isaac on Mount Moriah. (vv. 21-24, Gen. 22) His act of obedience confirmed he already possessed an unwavering faith which had taken root 30 years earlier when he believed God and God counted his belief as righteousness. (Gen. 15:6) That's when Abraham was saved; his actions on Mount Moriah were the marks that he was a man living by faith.

Rahab, the streetwalker turned saint, is James' second example. (v. 25) An enemy of God by birth, she was destined for destruction when Jericho fell. But in helping the Israelites, she showed the sincerity of her trust in the one true God. She was saved from certain judgment to become part of the lineage of Jesus! Rahab was not saved *because* she cleaned up her life—just the opposite. Her amazing transformation evidenced God's miraculous power working in and through her.

To reinforce his point, James uses the illustration of a corpse. A dead body can't move, talk, think, breathe or feel. But does the fact that your body can do those things make you alive? No. You're able to do those things *because* you have life. The actions demonstrate the inner dynamic. That's why James basically says, "I'll show you my faith by my works. You show me your faith *without* any works... and we'll bury it and apply a suitable epitaph."

Consider James' two examples of faith that works: the renowned and revered first Hebrew patriarch—and a disreputable pagan woman who was the first known Gentile convert. What insights can you draw from this?

_____
_____
_____
_____
_____
_____

Reflect on the time faith first took root in your heart and the transformations God has brought in your life since. Praise Him for His power at work in you today.

_____
_____
_____
_____
_____
_____

How could you see past empty words and rote religiosity to help someone recognize their genuine need for true faith in Christ?

_____
_____
_____
_____
_____

Help me to rest in Your grace and wait upon Your strength, Lord.

...walk worthy of the calling with which you were called, with all lowliness and gentleness, with longsuffering, bearing with one another in love...

Ephesians 4:1-2

The Christian life begins with resting. In order to be saved, we first have to stop trying and start trusting. And when our faith rests securely in the finished work of Jesus Christ, we're seated with Him in the heavenly places. (2:6) But after this rest, we're also called to a vocation: a worthy walk. Our faith is to have legs on it. In fact, we're told eight times in Ephesians to "walk." So we should consider what this particular word expresses.

"Walk" implies a *decision*. When you were saved, you chose to move in a certain direction, following Jesus and walking as He walked. (1 John 2:6) You have a *destination*. You're headed somewhere, maturing in your faith as you go. And in walking there's a *determination*. You haven't arrived yet, but you are steadily, deliberately progressing toward what God has for you.

We're called to serve the Lord day by day, step by step...which can prove to be the most difficult thing to do. Consider what God says in Isaiah 40:31: "But those who wait on the Lord shall renew *their* strength; they shall mount up with wings like eagles, they shall run and not be weary, they shall walk and not faint." This may seem to start with a highpoint and go down—from soaring to running to walking. But God didn't get the emphasis wrong. He knows that **walking** may be the *greatest* test of our strength. Some moments we can be caught up in worship and lifted to heavenly places, our spirits soaring! Other times we may find ourselves running with some task God has given, vigorously pressing forward to fulfill that purpose. But the hardest thing is to just keep plodding through the ordinary, everyday things of life—living out our faith day by day—*walking* and not fainting!

God has us begin our walk with Him by resting. He promises to then strengthen us to fulfill our calling as we rely upon Him. What blessings do you find in this?

_____
_____
_____
_____
_____

Consider the grace the Lord gives you and the glory to which you are called. How can this help you make it through the mundane with joy in your heart?

_____
_____
_____
_____
_____

Since we're also called to "bear with one another in love"—how could you help a fellow believer to "walk worthy"? What else does this passage reveal about how we should treat one another along the way?

_____
_____
_____
_____
_____

May my daily faith-walk be honoring to You, Lord.

As you therefore have **received Christ Jesus** the Lord, so **walk in Him.**

Colossians 2:6

You received the Lord Jesus by repentance and faith. That's just how you are to live the Christian life: keep repeating the process that brought you to Christ. You don't keep getting saved. But after you're saved, you don't stop repenting and you don't stop believing.

Repentance is turning *away* from self. Faith is turning *to* Jesus. As you move through your life in Christ, the Holy Spirit continues to reveal more about you and more about Him, constantly showing you your spiritual bankruptcy and the great riches of the Lord Jesus Christ. You don't want to miss out on the treasure hidden in Him! (vv. 2-3)

It doesn't say to walk *with* the Lord or *follow after* Him. You are to walk in Him. Jesus becomes the boundaries of your life. He is the circumference of your walk. But don't think you're somehow limited, fenced in by Him. That would be like a minnow being hemmed in by the Atlantic Ocean! There is nothing—absolutely nothing—worth having outside of Jesus Christ.

This verb *walk* literally means "to keep on walking." Walking *begins* with one step...but walking is a *series* of steps. If in your Christian life you take *a* step and that's all, you'll be off balance—as if you're standing with one foot poised precariously in the air, ready to take another step. You can stay that way for only so long. *The problem with many people is that they've stepped into Jesus and stopped. And they wonder why they don't have any balance.*

The Christian life is to be lived one step at a time: repentance and faith, repentance and faith, repentance and faith. The same way you first came into Christ. And you continue the process each day, all within the boundary of Jesus: "That you may **walk worthy** of the Lord, fully pleasing Him, being fruitful in every good work and increasing in the knowledge of God" (Col. 1:10).

Are you willing for Jesus to be the boundaries of your life, or does that sound stifling to you? Do you feel you have balance in your spiritual life, or are you uncertain of your next step?

When you go out into the world today, what can you do to ensure yours is a worthy walk?

Look at Colossians 2:2-3. What encouraging truths could you share with someone to help them discover the treasures that are theirs in Christ?

Open my heart and let me be completely honest with You, Lord.

Jesus answered and said to them, "Go and tell John the things which you hear and see: The blind see and the lame walk; the lepers are cleansed and the deaf hear; the dead are raised up and the poor have the gospel preached to them. And **blessed is he who is not offended because of Me.**"

MATTHEW 11:4-6

Of all the people ever born there was none greater than John the Baptist. (v. 11) That's what Jesus said about him just after He sent John's disciples back with an answer to his earnest question: "Are you really the Messiah?" (v. 3) It seems unthinkable that the mighty forerunner of Jesus—His own cousin, anointed by the Spirit from *before* birth—would ask such a thing! Yet John had a moment of doubt that almost turned into a grudge against God.

Have you ever been offended at God? Ever resented the way He's running the universe or been angry at some of the things He's done? Well, God is God. He doesn't need your forgiveness. But *you* may need to come to Him to rid yourself of bitterness that will eat away at you and corrode your relationship with the One Who knows and loves you best.

Suffering and disappointments can cause you to question God. For a year John had been cooped up in prison, unable to roam freely, preach fearlessly and fulfill the purpose for which he was created. While he was in a desolate place, he heard Jesus was going about doing good. Where was the Christ of judgment he'd been proclaiming? And if Jesus could do all these things for others, why didn't He get John out of prison? John began to have doubts, but they were honest doubts. And he took them to Jesus, Who gave him an honest answer. Come to Him in sincerity and Jesus will always do the same for you.

Jesus knew John was only having a lapse of faith. But in His answer, He was saying, "John, let me be God. Let me do it My way. Don't get upset when things don't go as you think they should." Sometimes it takes a lot of faith to let God be God. But trust Him—our Lord knows exactly what He is doing.

TAPESTRY

Are you holding onto some resentment toward God? Don't let anything cause you to doubt His power, His ability to work in your life or His love for you. Lay your heart before Him and let Him answer your earnest questions.

_____
_____
_____
_____
_____
_____

Any time you're tempted to question God, or how He is handling things, read Romans 11:33-36 and Isaiah 55:8-9 and reflect on Who God is.

_____
_____
_____
_____
_____
_____

What do you find here that could be an encouragement to someone you know who has encountered suffering or disappointments?

_____
_____
_____
_____
_____
_____

Thank You, Lord, for washing, sanctifying and justifying me!

> *By faith* the **harlot Rahab did not perish with those who did not believe**, *when she had received the spies with peace.*
>
> HEBREWS 11:31

Hebrews 11 is God's Hall of Fame for those He holds up as champions of faith. As a prostitute and part of a pagan race who were enemies of God's children, Rahab seems an unlikely candidate for this honor. But God saved this woman and radically, dramatically changed her. Never forget: our Lord is in the transformation business, and the greatest power on earth is the grace of God made available by faith.

A lady named Iris, a great soul winner known for her Christian witness, gave this testimony of the moment she prayed to receive Christ: "I got on my knees a filthy prostitute; I arose a virgin in the sight of God." If that seems impossible, consider what Paul says in 1 Corinthians 6:9-11:

> ...Neither fornicators, nor idolaters, nor adulterers, nor homosexuals... nor thieves, nor covetous, nor drunkards...nor extortioners will inherit the kingdom of God. And such **were** some of you. But you were washed... sanctified...justified in the name of our Lord Jesus...

Not such *are* some of you; such **were** some of you—before encountering God's grace. Nature forms us, sin deforms us, schools inform us, prisons reform us, the world conforms us...but Jesus transforms us by His indisputably ultimate power. And we are linked to that power through faith.

Christians are not just nicer people; we are absolutely new people. Think of Rahab: a pagan in spiritual darkness, a prostitute in sinful degradation and a Canaanite destined for sure destruction. Yet God saved Rahab and she became the great-great grandmother of King David—part of the bloodline of Jesus! No longer a child of hell, she's now a citizen of heaven. Once a shady lady walking the back streets of Jericho, now a celebrated saint in the house of God, dancing on streets of gold. That's the transforming power that is ours by faith!

Is there anything you think God cannot forgive you for? Anything you're reluctant to let go of? What is God calling you to do in response to this lesson?

_____
_____
_____
_____
_____
_____

What can you point to in your life as a testimony to God's transforming power?

_____
_____
_____
_____
_____

Again we're reminded no one is too "bad" for God to save. Select someone you think of as an unlikely candidate for salvation and begin to pray for them. Look for ways to reach out to the "unlovable"—who are precious in His sight.

_____
_____
_____
_____
_____

Open my heart to the truths You have for me today, Lord.

*"And as soon as **we heard these things**, our hearts melted...for **the Lord your God**, He is God in heaven above and on earth beneath."*

Joshua 2:11

This is quite a confession of faith...especially for a pagan prostitute whose people were the enemies of the men to whom she was speaking. How could Rahab have known that the God of Israel was the one true God over all? She'd heard what the Lord had done for His people. The inhabitants of Jericho knew about the victories God had piled upon the Israelites and the judgment He was dispensing through them as they came into the Promised Land.

The Holy Spirit of God convicts through people who are living in victory. Our lives should cause others to say, "I know there's a God because I can see what He's done for you." As Christians, the only right we have to ask anybody to believe anything we say is that they see in us something different. When we begin to live amazing lives, people will be asking, "What must we do to be saved?"

That's what Rahab wanted to know from the spies she'd hidden and protected. (vv. 12-13) She was hungry to know the Lord. It was not mere chance that brought these men to Rahab's house; it was divine providence. God saw that her heart was tender toward Him and sent messengers to share His Word. (Jam. 2:25) They were more than spies; they were spokesmen for Almighty God. In detailing how Rahab and her family could be spared, they were testifying of God's Passover Lamb and the shed blood necessary for salvation.

Rahab acted in faith to help the spies, but unashamedly hanging the scarlet cord in the window was also an act of faith—and obedience. (v. 21) She believed the truth she was given and acted upon it. And by the power of the blood that would be shed on Calvary, Rahab and her family were saved and she was transformed from the shady lady of Jericho into a princess of Israel.

Ask yourself: "Would anybody fall under conviction because of my life?" What more could you do to reflect what the Lord has done for you?

_____
_____
_____
_____
_____
_____

Of all the other people in Jericho who knew about the God of Israel, only Rahab responded with such conviction. What do think this says about hearts that are hungry for the Lord?

_____
_____
_____
_____
_____
_____

If you viewed those around you as people you might spend eternity with, how could it help you share God's love?

_____
_____
_____
_____
_____
_____

Help me to lay hold of the blessed reality You have for me today, Lord.

*Now **faith is the substance of things hoped for**, the evidence of things not seen.*

HEBREWS 11:1

The word translated *faith* here may also be translated "belief" or "trust." The whole person is involved in this matter of faith: it requires the mind to believe, the emotions to trust, and the will to take action. What happens is this: God speaks to your heart and there is heartfelt agreement. You say, "That is truth!" Agreeing with the truth resounding in your heart leads to an attitude of trust. You say, "I know it to be so." Finally, you act upon that trust. At last you have true, Biblical faith.

Agreement—hearing God speak to your heart and in your spirit, you say, "Amen. It is true." **Attitude**—you trust; commit to that truth. **Action**—you do something about it. Hebrews 11 is the most action-packed chapter in the Bible, showing what so many did by faith. We see that faith is belief with legs on it. It *does* something.

But Bible faith doesn't just step out in uncertainty. The word *substance* here is very much alike in Greek and English. *Sub* means something beneath you; *stance* means something firm, something you can stand on. When you're trusting God, you're not walking around on egg shells but on something substantial—on spiritual steel and concrete. And when the Bible speaks of hope, it means a divine certainty based on a sure Word from God. Things hoped for are those things God has promised. So you could really read this verse this way: "Faith is the reality of things expected."

Faith gives you the ability to make present substance out of future reality. When you know the things God has promised, you have the assurance they will come to pass. You can count on them as if they had already happened. Faith reaches out and brings the future into the present, grasping what is yet to be seen and making it real—substantive in your heart and in your life.

TAPESTRY

What promises of God do you need to reach out to and bring into your present day reality? How can you make them substantive in your heart and life?

Try these words from other Bible translations in place of the word *substance*: "assurance," "confidence," "guarantee," or "the title deed." What more does this say to you about counting on—and acting upon—God's promises?

What did you find here that can help you minister to someone who is struggling with uncertainty and needs some spiritual steel and concrete to stand on?

Lord, help me to keep an eternal perspective throughout each day.

*Now **faith is** the substance of things hoped for, the **evidence of things not seen.***

Hebrews 11:1

Faith not only reaches out to what is *yet* to be seen, it also substantiates what is unseen in the here and now. The world says: "What you see is what you get," and "Seeing is believing." The Bible says just the opposite when it comes to faith. What you *don't* see is what you get, and believing is seeing.

There is an unseen world that is very, very real: "By faith we understand that the worlds were framed by the word of God, so that the things which are seen were not made of things which are visible" (Heb. 11:3). You can rephrase that last part to say, "What you *can* see was made out of things you *can't* see." We know this is true of the molecular structure of the universe. Everything is made of miniscule atoms we really cannot see. Many of us have electronic devices that allow us to pull music, movies, newscasts and any number of things right out of the air. All of those things are there around us, we just can't see them.

In many ways, the unseen world is more real than the visible world. The invisible world was here first and it will be here last: "...For the things which are seen are temporary, but the things which are not seen are eternal" (2 Cor. 4:18). That which you cannot see is that which lasts forever. As believers we should maintain an eternal perspective. We need faith to see the invisible so we can know the unknowable and do the impossible.

That doesn't mean we can *believe* something into being. Our faith evidences what is already there, according to the promises of God. Positive thinking says, "If I believe hard enough, *it'll be so.*" The Bible says, "*It is so.* Believe it!"...even if you don't see it.

Faith enables us to treat the future as present and the invisible as seen. How could maintaining this perspective change your outlook on life?

There's more to life than what we can see, touch, taste, smell, or hear. What are you doing to hone your sense of faith each day?

Think of what you can do to always keep an eternal perspective and consider how it will help you in reaching out to others.

May I take up my cross, Lord, that You might live through me.

---

*I have been crucified with Christ; **it is no longer I who live**, but **Christ lives in me**; and the life which I now live in the flesh **I live by faith in the Son of God**, Who loved me and **gave Himself** for me.*

Galatians 2:20

Most of us know we're saved by Jesus and His death on the cross and we can't do anything to save ourselves. But then we think maturing in our faith is something *we* have to do. As Paul said to the Galatians, "How foolish!" (3:1) We're saved by trusting in Christ and only by faith can we be sanctified to *become* like Him. Sanctification is how God saves us day by day from self, sin and Satan and makes us more and more like Jesus through the principle of the cross.

To follow Him, Jesus said we must take up our cross. Crosses are not for carrying; crosses are for dying on. It was an invitation to come and die. Look closely at what Jesus said: "...'If anyone desires to come after Me, let him deny himself, and take up his cross daily, and follow Me. For whoever desires to save his life will lose it, but whoever loses his life for My sake will save it'" (Luke 9:23-24). Jesus promises abundant life—but the cross is the way to that life. Only one life has power: the crucified life. The principle of the cross means letting that old self die with Christ and allowing Him to take over and live through you.

Maybe you've spent much of your Christian life in a cycle of trying and failing. You *try* to serve God, but it's like being in quicksand. The more you struggle, the more you sink. Each time you ask forgiveness and vow to do better, you end up failing yet again. It's time to stop trying and start trusting. Consider yourself crucified with Christ, dead to sin but alive to God. Just say, "Lord, as I trusted You to save me, I'm now trusting You to make me what You want me to be." The same Jesus Who died to save you and gave Himself *for* you is the One Who rose to give Himself *to* you and will live *in* and *through* you if you'll let Him!

Not only do we need to come to the cross for pardon; we need to get on the cross for the power to live the Christian life. What is God saying to you today about responding to these truths?

_____
_____
_____
_____
_____
_____

Jesus willingly, voluntarily took up His cross, and so must you. How do you envision this translating into practical action in your daily life

_____
_____
_____
_____
_____
_____

Do you know someone who's stuck in spiritual quicksand—trying harder and harder and sinking deeper and deeper? How could you reach out to help them?

_____
_____
_____
_____
_____
_____

I pray You will give me spiritual wisdom as I rely upon You, Lord.

Through faith we understand that the worlds were framed by the Word of God, so that things which are seen were not made of things which do appear.

HEBREWS 11:3

There are things you will never understand apart from faith. Faith is the dynamic of spiritual wisdom. In the Bible, God is not explained. God is not argued. God is simply presented. And that is how He must be accepted—simply by faith: "...for he that comes to God must believe that He is..." (v. 6).

The skeptic will challenge you to prove there is a God. Don't ever try to do that. The finite cannot prove the infinite. Just say, "Well, I can't do it." And as he smirks smugly, you can say, "Now prove there is no God." Of course, he can't do it. The skeptic accepts **by faith** there is no God. **All people are believers.** There are those who believe in God and those who believe there is no God, but all are believers.

Science is the study of phenomena now existing. Back in the oldest book of the Bible, God asked Job, "'Where were you when I laid the foundations of the earth? Tell Me, if you have understanding'" (Job 38:4). No scientists were there. There's no way they can explain it. How do we understand it? By faith. Some say, "Well, that takes a lot of belief." *Really?* Seems a lot more belief is required to assert that nothing times nobody equals everything. That's what they choose to believe. No wonder the Bible says, "The fool has said in his heart, 'There is no God'..." (Psa. 53:1). God is the supreme fact, and the man who denies the supreme fact is the supreme fool.

Remember, faith is not contrary to reason; it's simply beyond reason. To go into the laboratory to try to prove God would be like tearing apart a piano to try to find a tune. It's impossible...just as it is impossible to have spiritual wisdom without faith.

Is the fact that all people are believers a new thought for you to consider? What lessons can you take from these insights to apply to your life?

_____
_____
_____
_____
_____
_____

In what ways do you rely upon spiritual wisdom in your everyday life? How could you learn from Job and grow your faith?

_____
_____
_____
_____
_____
_____

Are there skeptics you encounter on a regular basis? How could you use the truths here to speak lovingly to those who doubt God's existence and help them see that they need to redirect their faith?

_____
_____
_____
_____
_____
_____

Open my heart, Lord, to respond to You in all Your glory.

>Then He said to Thomas, "Reach your finger here, and look at My hands; and reach your hand here, and put it into My side. **Do not be unbelieving**, but believing." And Thomas answered and said to Him, "My Lord and my God!" Jesus said to him, "Thomas, because you have seen Me, you have believed. **Blessed are those who have not seen and yet have believed**."
>
> JOHN 20:27-29

Thomas demanded proof before he would believe. But God is not obligated to prove Himself to us. Faith is not a response to proof. Faith is the heart's response to the character of God.

Jesus Christ left all of His splendor and glory in heaven and came to earth as a very ordinary-looking man. The Bible says there was nothing about His appearance to make Him stand out in any way. (Isa. 53:2) Do you think Jesus looked the way He's often depicted—like He just stepped out of a beauty salon, wearing flowing robes, with a glowing dinner plate behind His head? If that's how He looked, why would Judas have to point Him out so the soldiers could take Him away? He was physically very nondescript. Yet in Him there was supreme glory, serenity, dignity, majesty, purity—all of the character of God in human flesh without any outward extravagance. And when He did miracles they were not publicity stunts. He didn't advertise them. The acts themselves simply attested to the fact that He was Who He said He was.

Why did He come as He did? Because He wanted what He wanted...and that was faith. He could buy us, bribe us or convince us. He could give some instantaneous, miraculous proof to cause us to believe. He doesn't want that. He wants hearts to respond to His true divine character. When your eye is right, it responds to light. When your ear is right, it responds to sound. When your heart is right it responds to God and that response is called "faith."

Consider Thomas' doubt and what Jesus said to him about those who believe without having seen. What lesson do you find in this for your life?

_____
_____
_____
_____
_____
_____

Spend time reflecting on the character of God. Think of specific attributes like His holiness, kindness, faithfulness and omnipotence—or how He is patient, merciful, loving and righteous. How does this deepen your faith?

_____
_____
_____
_____
_____
_____

What truths could you share with someone who needs to learn to rely on faith and not sight?

_____
_____
_____
_____
_____
_____

Allow me to see the truth You have for me here today, Lord.

For **Christ** *also* **suffered once for sins, the just for the unjust***, that He might bring us to God, being put to death in the flesh but made alive by the Spirit.*

1 Peter 3:18

This verse is so packed with Gospel dynamite that a spark of faith can set it off in your heart and blow away the sin, hatred and disappointment, transforming your life! How does God forgive sin? This verse provides the powerful answer. First, we need to dispel some popular misguided thinking and realize exactly Who forgives sin.

Suppose someone punches you in the nose. You decide to be bighearted about it, so you say, "Well, even though you punched me in the nose, I forgive you." But that person says, "You don't need to forgive me. I've already forgiven myself." As strange as that would be, suppose a third person sees the two of you talking and says, "Hey, don't worry about who's going to forgive who. I've already forgiven you both." What's he got to do with it? The only one who needs to do any forgiving is the one who got punched, right?

Some misconceptions today have people affirming themselves or trying to affirm others with an "I'm okay, you're okay" mentality. But it is **God** Who has been offended. And we're the ones who have morally struck Him. We don't just forgive ourselves. Someone else cannot forgive us. **God** must forgive us, because this sin is against Him alone. (Psa. 51:4)

We are sinners by birth, by nature, by choice and by practice. And God in His holiness has no choice but to punish sin. So how does God handle this, when He loves us and wants to fellowship with us, but there's the matter of our offense against Him? It took a substitutionary sacrifice—Someone blameless Who was willing to take the punishment on our behalf. The only One Who could do that was the sinless Son of God Himself. Jesus actually *took our place*. He died not merely *for* us...He died *instead* of us. Never forget the freedom and forgiveness you've been granted in Christ!

Tapestry

Think of the Father's love for you and how Jesus willingly took the punishment you deserved. How does this affect you?

_____
_____
_____
_____
_____
_____

Have you ever thought of your sins as a punch in the face to God? How might it help you avoid sin in your daily life if you thought of each instance as a painful assault on Him?

_____
_____
_____
_____
_____
_____

What did you find here that you could share to help someone appreciate the substitutionary sacrifice Jesus made for them?

_____
_____
_____
_____
_____
_____

Thank You for seeking me out and forgiving me, Lord.

*And be kind to one another, tenderhearted, **forgiving** one another, even as God in Christ forgave you.*

ЕPHESIANS 4:32

Forgiveness is the canceling of a debt and when you forgive your debtor, you must tear up his I.O.U. It may be extremely costly. Remember, the model for forgiving is God Himself. How you were forgiven is the way you are to forgive. That means you are to forgive freely, eagerly and quickly.

Some people forgive *after* they've collected their revenge. They want the person who wronged them to know how badly they've been hurt. So they criticize, castigate, scold, freeze out—do everything they can to cause that individual to squirm like a worm in hot ashes. Finally, after they've exacted their pound of flesh, they say, "Well, I forgive you." The person being "*forgiven*" feels like saying, "Never mind. I've already paid!" You are to forgive freely, not after you've made someone pay a hefty price.

Because you forgive freely, you're to be quick about it. If you're not in a hurry to forgive, the bitterness you feel will become an infection and your wound will be much more difficult to heal. All bitterness is to be put away from us. The Bible teaches that we're to be so anxious to forgive a brother or sister that we are to seek them out—literally *run after them*—to forgive them. (Mat. 18:15)

Whether you're in the right or in the wrong, whether you have something against your brother or you know your brother has something against you, you are to take the offensive and go to that individual. Isn't that what God did in the Garden of Eden? Adam and Eve sinned against God, yet God came into the garden and cried out, "Adam, where are you?" (Gen. 3:9) That was not the voice of a detective. It was the voice of broken-hearted Father seeking His children—longing to be reconciled to them. You're to seek out the one who has wronged you in the same way and be in a hurry to forgive.

Here is a motto to live by: "Keep a short account with God and with men." How will this have an effect on you if you apply it in your everyday life?

_____
_____
_____
_____
_____
_____

Have you ever "forgiven" someone...after exacting a price from them? Aren't you glad this is not how God extends forgiveness to us? Think of how this perspective could change the way you treat those who have wronged you.

_____
_____
_____
_____
_____
_____

What could you share with someone else to help them open up to hear God calling them to enjoy a relationship with Him?

_____
_____
_____
_____
_____
_____

Focus my heart and mind on what You want to reveal to me, Lord.

*"Moreover if your brother sins against you, go and tell him his fault between you and him alone. If he hears you, **you have gained your brother**."*

Matthew 18:15

By choosing to forgive, not only do you lose those things that have wounded you, but you gain your brother. The person who has wronged you is either a brother or a potential brother; a sister or a potential sister. That is a precious thing. The Bible says, "Behold, how good and how pleasant it is for brethren to dwell together in unity!" (Psa.133:1).

How sad it is when brothers and sisters fail to forgive. It disgraces the Father when God's children do not love one another. And it discourages the saints. Few things hurt a church worse than an unforgiving spirit. It also dissuades the lost. Unsaved people are quick to see when there is a rift in a family, a tear in the fellowship. They're quick to point it out, and many of them are not saved because of the sin in our hearts and lives. That's why the Devil more than anyone else delights to see brethren with an unforgiving spirit.

And if the person who has sinned against you is not a sister or brother in Christ but an unbeliever—all the more reason he should be the object of your mercy. Because not only has he done wrong, but if he's an unbeliever he's blind and does not have the grace and power you have. If he is a brother, you are in the same Body. And when you harm him, you harm you. He's to be the object of your love. If he's not a brother, he's lost and on his way to hell and you don't need to drive him further that way. He needs *more* of your love. The person you forgive is more than a person who hurt you. He or she is a person who needs you. They need to experience the grace of God just as you have. We have everything to gain, nothing to lose, by forgiving someone else.

Do you need to repent of the sin of unforgiveness that could be harming a brother or sister or keeping others from coming to Christ? What is God's Spirit revealing to you today?

_____
_____
_____
_____
_____
_____

How might it affect the way you respond to others if you realized their need for grace and saw them as a potential sister or brother in Christ?

_____
_____
_____
_____
_____
_____

Have you ever thought that your forgiveness could be a witnessing tool? What unsaved person could benefit from seeing God's mercy and grace in how you openly and freely forgive them?

_____
_____
_____
_____
_____
_____

May I joyfully trust Your Word, Your way and Your will for me, Lord.

Now **the Lord had said** *to Abram: "Get out of your country, from your family and from your father's house,* **to a land that I will show you.** *I will make you a great nation;* **I will** *bless you and* **make your name great...""**

GENESIS 12:1-2

Abraham is called "the father of all those who believe" (Rom. 4:11). In the School of Faith, he would be the Dean. And we would do well to make ourselves students of his example.

The basis for Abraham's faith was divine revelation; God had spoken to him. The source of faith is often misunderstood. It's not rooted in human will. The Tower of Babel was a futile attempt of man to establish his own kingdom by his own means. The people there had a specific, stated goal: "Let *us* make *us* a name" (Gen. 11:4). But are the names of any of those people known today? They failed miserably. But **God** said to Abraham, "**I will** make your name great," and the name Abraham is revered throughout the world.

Faith is not rooted in human wisdom; it's not figuring something out and then trying to make it work. When Abraham went out from his homeland, he didn't know why and he didn't know where; he only knew Whom. Faith does not rest on a roadmap but in a relationship with Almighty God. If you're not connected to Him, hearing Him speak to you, you're not living by faith. It's impossible. You're just going here and there, doing whatever *you think* you ought to do. But that's still a Tower of Babel mentality—like many today who go around naming things they want and then trying to claim them. But you can't "name it and claim it." You must *believe it and receive it* after hearing from God.

Acting upon what God has said requires you to come out of where you are and go to where you need to be, just as Abraham did. Many people try to have faith right where they are in their same old lifestyle...and they wonder why it doesn't work. There's nothing more deadening to faith than sin. If you're having trouble with faith, try repentance.

What specific lessons for your life can you draw from Abraham's example of faith?

_____
_____
_____
_____
_____
_____

How are you working to develop your relationship with the Lord? What are you doing to get to know Him more and hear Him better each day?

_____
_____
_____
_____
_____
_____

What truths do you find here that you could share with someone to help them move from just believing God to actually acting upon His Word for them?

_____
_____
_____
_____
_____
_____
_____

Please allow Your mighty river of blessings to flow through me and on to others, Lord.

"I will make you a great nation; **I will bless you** *and make your name great;* **and you shall be a blessing.** *I will bless those who bless you, and I will curse him who curses you; and* **in you all the families of the earth shall be blessed."**

Genesis 12:2-3

By faith Abraham received a blessing. He stepped out into the unknown because he believed God, and as God began fulfilling His promise to Abraham, a river of blessings began to flow that has reached us today—and continues without end in sight.

Hebrews 11:6 tells us that God rewards those who diligently seek Him and that we please God when we believe Him. By faith man gives God pleasure and by faith God gives man treasure. Not just *some* but **every** blessing of God is appropriated by faith. You're saved by faith and you live the Christian life by faith.

But notice Abraham was blessed *that he might be a blessing*. Faith enables us to receive blessings and also empowers us to bless others. The problem with many people is that they want faith sort of as a Midas touch, just so they can get what they want. Their desire is purely self-centered and they're destined to stagnate in their selfishness. God wants you to be a river of revival, not a reservoir of blessings. If you begin to pray like this, "God, bless me and make me a blessing," then faith will begin to flow through your life.

It's amazing how much God will let pass through your hands if you'll receive and give, just letting His blessings come through. And you'll be so incredibly blessed when you are blessing others. Have you ever thought of how we are blessed today because of Abraham? Out of Abraham came the Jewish nation. We have the descendants of Abraham who gave us the Bible. We have Moses and the prophets. Above all, from Abraham's lineage we received the Incarnation—God in human flesh—the Lord Jesus Christ. There is no greater blessing than to be a blessing. That's the reward of faith.

God is still fulfilling His promise to Abraham today—blessing *all the families of the earth.* How does this motivate you?

_____
_____
_____
_____
_____
_____

Think of some of the people God has used to bless you. As you thank Him for those special individuals, think of ways you might also be a blessing to others. Ask God to open your life to allow His blessings to flow through you.

_____
_____
_____
_____
_____
_____

What is the Holy Spirit revealing to you about how you could help someone else by passing on these truths—or by specifically blessing them in some way?

_____
_____
_____
_____
_____
_____

Don't let me block the flow of Your forgiveness in my life, Lord.

*"For **if you forgive** men their trespasses, **your heavenly Father will also forgive you**. But **if you do not forgive** men their trespasses, **neither will your Father forgive** your trespasses."*

MATTHEW 6:14-15

According to what Jesus says here, if you withhold forgiveness from someone else after having been forgiven by God...you dam up the stream of His forgiveness. And that stream stops until you are willing to forgive that one who has sinned against you.

One man said, "I had a hard time forgiving people until I decided I wasn't going to fall out with anyone until they treated me worse than I treated Jesus." We crucified the Lord Jesus Christ. We have clearly experienced the grace of God and we must allow that grace to flow through us to others. God says we must forgive others as we have been forgiven; therefore an unforgiving spirit is unforgivable. The person who will not forgive destroys the bridge over which he himself must travel.

These verses directly follow the Lord's Prayer. Have you ever thought of how dangerous this prayer is? This model prayer Jesus gave to show us how to approach our heavenly Father says, "And forgive us our debts as we forgive our debtors" (v. 11). When you pray this, what you've said is, "God, treat me like I treat other people. Forgive me the same way I forgive others."

Just how *do* you forgive others? Maybe you say, "I forgive her but I'll never have anything more to do with her." God says "All right, I'll forgive you and never have anything more to do with you." You say "Well, I'll forgive, but I can't forget." God says, "All right, I forgive you but I won't forget." And if you simply won't forgive at all, then you're effectively cutting off God's forgiveness in your own life. Careful what you pray—do you really want God to deal with you the way you deal with other people?

TAPESTRY

Examine how you forgive others to see if there is anything blocking God's forgiveness in your life—or keeping Him from fellowshipping with you, or preventing Him from putting your sins completely behind His back.

___

Look at Matthew 6:5-15 to see all that Jesus instructed about how we should pray, then apply these verses to your life in context.

___

We are all sinners hopelessly indebted to God. How can you reach out to someone to share how Jesus paid the debt for them to be forgiven and free?

___

Thank You for patiently reminding me to simply trust You, Lord.

Jesus answered and said to them, "**This is the work of God**, *that you* **believe in Him** *whom He sent.*"

John 6:29

Before the term *Christians* was ever used, early followers of Christ were known as *believers*. That's how they were defined. Faith is the distinguishing mark of the Christian. No one has a right to call themselves a Christian who is not a believer. It's our description and our duty to believe.

Once you believe on the Lord Jesus Christ, how are you intended to live the Christian life? By trying? No. By trusting. "The just shall live by faith" is such an important truth, it's repeated multiple times in the Bible: Habakkuk 2:4, Romans 1:17, Galatians 3:11, and Hebrews 10:38. Do you think God is trying to tell us something? Maybe He wants us to remember: *the way to live the Christian life is* **by faith.**

The only way you'll overcome this world is by faith: "And this is the victory that has overcome the world—our faith. Who is he who overcomes the world, but he who believes that Jesus is the Son of God?" (1 John 5:4-5).

Your success in your Christian life is going to be measured by your faith. "...According to your faith let it be to you" (Mat. 9:29). Not according to your feeling, your fame, your fortune, your friends, your fate, but according to your faith, Jesus said.

Faith above all things pleases God—in fact, it's impossible to please Him without it. (Heb. 11: 6) If you please God, it doesn't matter whom you displease; and if you displease God, it doesn't matter whom you please.

Our chief calling, the way we do the work of God, is to exercise faith. When we greet fellow Christians, rather than saying, "How are you feeling?", we should say, "How are you *faithing*?" because we need to hold one another accountable for living as true believers. Not only do we need to possess a faith...we need a faith that possesses us.

Could it really be as simple as taking God at His Word and just returning to reliance on Him whenever we forget to walk by faith? If so, why do you think God repeated Himself so many times about how to live the Christian life?

_____
_____
_____
_____
_____
_____

How are *you* "faithing" today? Where are you fulfilling your duty as a Christian, trusting God and acting in obedience to what He shows?

_____
_____
_____
_____
_____
_____

Maybe someone you know needs to be reminded: *the way to live the Christian life is by faith*. How could you come alongside a struggling friend and encourage them with today's truths?

_____
_____
_____
_____
_____
_____

Help me to see unbelief in my own life as something that blocks others from seeing Your glory in me, Lord.

---

*"He who believes in Him is not condemned; but he **who does not believe is condemned** already, **because he has not believed** in the name of the only begotten Son of God."*

JOHN 3:18

The Bible tells us that unbelief is a supreme evil. It was unbelief that led Eve to fall in the Garden of Eden. Unbelief kept the children of Israel out of the Promised Land for forty years. It is unbelief that sends men and women to hell. People don't go to hell because they lie, steal, or commit adultery; those sins have been paid for with the precious blood of Jesus. People die and go to hell because they have not believed on the Lord Jesus Christ.

There's no greater sin than to aim the gun of unbelief at God and pull the trigger. Unbelief is a slander against the character of God. "...He who does not believe God has made Him a liar..." (1 John 5:10). Unbelief says, "God, You cannot be trusted. *If You exist*, You're not a trustworthy god."

Unbelief never comes out of the head; it comes out of the heart. It is not an intellectual but a spiritual matter. That's why the Bible warns, "Beware, brethren, lest there be in any of you an evil heart of unbelief..." (Heb. 3:12). No one can use the excuse that they just *can't* believe, because the Lord has dealt to every man a measure of faith. (Rom. 12:3)

Faith is a gift of God, but God will not force you to believe. Breathing is a gift of God, because God gives you lungs and God gives you air. But you can smother if you want. And you can fail to believe God. The fault is yours. If you don't believe, it's not because you cannot; it is because you will not.

What we believe we live by. Don't prattle about your belief in a good God, a strong God, and then fail to believe Him. We are to live day-by-day by faith. And the Bible says to those who believe, nothing is impossible. To those who fail to believe, nothing is possible in the spiritual realm.

Look at John 3:16-18 altogether. What are some of the blessings God has made possible to all who believe? What is revealed about the sin of unbelief?

Have you ever considered how it reflects upon God when you claim to believe Him but fail to live in faith? What areas of your everyday life are shadowed by unbelief, keeping others from seeing the glory of God in you?

Do you know anyone who says they just aren't able to believe when it comes to spiritual things? How could you share about the gift of faith God gives to all?

Lord, help me never to be ashamed of my faith in You.

———⊸◆⊷———

That if you **confess** *with your mouth* **the Lord Jesus** *and* **believe** *in your heart that* **God has raised Him from the dead***, you will be saved. For* **with the heart one believes** *unto righteousness, and* **with the mouth confession is made** *unto salvation. For the Scripture says, "Whoever believes on Him will not be put to shame."*

Romans 10:9-11

Confession is faith turned inside out. When a person believes with their heart, they're always willing to confess with their mouth. Some say salvation is a private matter. The heart is private. But the mouth is public. And the Bible says that which happens in the inner sanctum of your heart will be evident on the outside if it's real. The faith that will not lead to confession will not lead to heaven.

Believing with the heart saves us; confession with the mouth shows we're saved. What are we to confess? The literal language of this verse says "Jesus is Lord." This is the **conviction** of salvation: that Jesus Christ is Lord. When you're ready to say, "No longer am I ruler in my own life. Lord Jesus, by faith I enthrone You. Take control of my life and make me the person You want me to be." That is the **commitment** of salvation.

And the commitment is rooted in this **confidence**: we know that Jesus is Lord because God has raised Him from the dead. His divine sovereignty is proven by His miraculous resurrection. (Rom. 1:4) That is the capstone miracle—if you believe in the resurrection, you believe in the incarnation and the crucifixion and all the rest about Jesus. And when you believe that Jesus Christ walked out of that grave, what confidence that gives!

Having this confidence brings tremendous **courage**. If we believe Jesus has been raised from the dead and He is Lord of all, sovereign God, can we be ashamed of Him? One way you can know that you really believe in Jesus Christ is that you're not ashamed to openly confess your faith in Him as Lord and Savior— not just in church, but every day, everywhere you go.

Would it thrill you to be able to openly confess Christ or is that something you'd shy away from? What insights challenged you today and how will they help you grow your faith?

___

Think of how you speak frequently with warmth and enthusiasm about someone you love or admire. Do you speak about Jesus just as eagerly...as lovingly...as frequently? How is He being acknowledged in your daily life?

___

What's one thing you know about Jesus from personal experience that you'd be excited to share with someone? How could you find opportunities to "brag on the Lord" and let others know the reason for your confident faith?

___

Help me examine my heart, Lord, to make sure I love You above all.

By faith Abraham, **when he was tested**, *offered up Isaac, and he who had received the promises* **offered up his only begotten son**...

Hebrews 11:17

God wants to make your faith strong and pure, so He will give you some trials, some tests to see if your faith is real. He means you no harm—He simply wants you to know whether or not you have the real thing. God knows where you are; He'll send trials tailor-made for your circumstances.

You may be surprised to find Him testing you—not by asking you to give up the *bad* things, but the *good* things. The real question is not are you willing to give up your sins for God, but are you able to give your blessings back to God? That's what Abraham was asked to do. Genesis 22:1-14 tells the incredible story of Abraham's test of faith when God told him to put his beloved son, Isaac, to death. God had never before commanded human sacrifice. And Isaac was the son of a miracle birth, the promised son on whom hinged all the plans God had laid out for Abraham's future.

There are some things we give up for the Lord. But Abraham's test was in what he was being asked to *give back* to the Lord. Why the test? Perhaps Abraham was coming to love Isaac more than he loved God—to love the gift more than the Giver. God will never take second place in our lives to anything or anyone. It was not wrong for Abraham to love his son. What God wanted to know was, "Abraham, do you love Me *more* than you love Isaac?" The test of faith is not primarily between love and hate, but between two loves: those things we love dearly and the One we must love supremely.

Do you have in your heart any love that is greater than your love for Jesus? Is there anything God has given to you that you would not willingly give back to Him if He asked you for it? If you're struggling with a test of faith like this, remember: anything God has given to you, you can trust Him with. And anything God has not given to you, you don't need.

As you read 1 Peter 1:6-9, what encouraging promises do you find for your own life?

___
___
___
___
___
___

Write out some of God's gifts to you that you're most thankful for. Look at each one as you contemplate those two closing questions. Pray over your list, asking God to help you truly trust Him with the possessions He has given you.

___
___
___
___
___
___

What truths from this lesson could you share with a friend who might be trying to bear up under some trials and testing in their life?

___
___
___
___
___
___

May I hear Your voice, Lord, and seek the purposes You have for me.

*...**God tested Abraham**, and said to him..."Take now your son, your only son Isaac, whom you love, and go to the land of Moriah, and offer him there as a burnt offering on one of the mountains of which I shall tell you." So **Abraham rose early** in the morning and...**went to the place of which God had told him**.*

GENESIS 22:1-3

Abraham was a man who acted upon what God told him. God had given him a purpose, a plan for his life. He could envision how it would all unfold: he would have a son; this son would have sons...ultimately there would be countless descendants—people of faith through whom the whole world would be blessed. A tremendous legacy and promise. So it didn't make sense when God said, "Put it to death."

Faith is not primarily believing God in spite of the evidence. It is obeying God in spite of the consequences. Obedience is the great proof of our trust and our faith. When we know *that we know* we have a word from God, we simply obey—not reluctantly, not moderately, not carelessly—but purposefully and passionately, as Abraham did.

Abraham heard God speaking. We must hear God in order to obey God. It is "informed" obedience that we're to have. To just make some sort of sacrifice to show God how much you love Him could be a horrible mistake. God has not promised to bless any endeavor He has not commanded.

And we must listen with the intent of responding readily to what we hear from Him. Ignorance of God's will is not an excuse. Real obedience is not merely abstaining from doing wrong. It is actively seeking the will of God for your life. Do you report to God for duty each day, ready to act upon His direction?

Abraham didn't hesitate to obey God, though He asked the unimaginable of him. Responding with informed, intentional and immediate obedience, he passed the test of his faith splendidly.

Is there anything God might ask of you that you'd be unwilling to do? Could you obey even if what He asked seemed contrary His plan for you?

_____
_____
_____
_____
_____
_____

Have you ever purposed to do something for God without consulting Him first? What can you do to be intentional about obeying His purposes for you each day?

_____
_____
_____
_____
_____
_____

Consider what it might do for the faith of someone else to see you responding to God without hesitation, even when things don't make sense.

_____
_____
_____
_____
_____
_____

Help me to trust You to keep the promises You have made, Lord.

By faith...he who had received the promises offered up his only begotten son, of whom it was said, "In Isaac your seed shall be called," **concluding that God was able** *to raise him up, even* **from the dead, from which he also received him** *in a figurative sense*

Hebrews 11:17-19

How could Abraham take the son of promise God had given him, lay him on an altar, and prepare to offer him as a burnt sacrifice? Killing Isaac would be antithetical to the promise—and Abraham dearly loved his son! So how was he able to look past these things and obey God in such a difficult test? He took inventory of what he knew and chose to trust God.

Abraham had already learned that God is the God of the impossible because God had given him a son when he was 100 years old and Sarah was 90. He knew that God is a God of miracles. And his faith was steadfast to believe God for the life of his son. He didn't know *how* God would do it. He just knew that God *would* do it.

The word *concluding* here literally means "to calculate." It's the Greek root of the words "logistics" and "logic." Abraham took account of what he knew to be true and came to a logical conclusion. He reckoned this way: "God, You gave me this boy; I can trust You with him. You have a purpose; I can trust You with it. Lord, You made a promise. I count on it. You're going to keep Your word. You cannot lie. I don't have to understand. I will just trust You and obey." And God gave him back his son. "And Abraham called the name of the place, The-Lord-Will-Provide..." (Gen. 22:14).

God did not let Abraham sacrifice Isaac. He provided a ram to take Isaac's place. For it wasn't Isaac that God wanted; it was Abraham. When he responded with such astounding obedience, God said, "Now I know that you love Me more than you love anything else." And God kept His promise to Abraham. (Heb. 11:12) Remember, we don't live by explanations, but by promises. And God wants us to have strong faith to rely on His promises.

In what recent ways has God provided for your needs? Take some time to praise and thank Him as you reflect now on these things.

_____
_____
_____
_____
_____

With the gifts He gives us, God can be trusted to fulfill His purposes in our lives and to keep His promises. What will you do to remain mindful of these truths as you encounter trials in your daily life?

_____
_____
_____
_____
_____

Think of how you can you reach out to someone today to remind them of God's promises and that we don't have to understand to trust Him.

_____
_____
_____
_____
_____

Give me strength to keep my eyes on You, Lord.

*Then Samson called to the LORD, saying, "O LORD God, **remember me, I pray! Strengthen me, I pray, just this once**, O God..."*

JUDGES 16:28

Samson was renowned for phenomenal physical strength—supernatural strength which had left him when he took his eyes off of the LORD. From a place of utter weakness, this once-great man of God recalled his faith and turned once more to the Source of his strength.

Never has there been a greater failure than Samson. Consecrated from birth, destined to help deliver his people from the Philistines (Jdg. 13:5), he was judge over Israel for twenty years. Also gifted with wisdom and wit, he was the hero of his day. But Samson went from hero to zero as sin took its tragic toll in his life. He spiraled from disobedience to defeat to disgrace and finally destruction. This man meant to bring God's deliverance was blinded, shackled and put on display by the Philistines as testament to the strength of *their* god! Once a dedicated servant of the LORD, empowered by His Spirit, Samson was bringing disgrace to the name of Jehovah God!

Remorseful, Samson began to reflect. He thought of God's great love for him, of His mercies and His willingness to forgive. He had enough faith to know that even though he was a failure and a disgrace—though he'd shamed God and forsaken His purposes—God still loved him and would remember him when he came in repentance and faith. *That's a lot of faith.* But our God truly is the God of the second chance. Honoring Samson's faith, He strengthened him one last time. In his death, Samson dealt a heavy blow to the enemies of God, killing 3,000 Philistines when he toppled their pagan temple. And this is why Samson is listed with the heroes of the faith. (Heb. 11:32)

No matter how you may have failed, God loves you. In spite of your faults, He accepts you. **Faith is our acceptance of God's acceptance of us.** The same forgiving God Who blessed Samson and chose him as an illustration of faith can restore you, bless you and help you learn to face failure with faith!

In what ways is Samson's physical strength illustrative of the spiritual strength the Holy Spirit provides today? How could faith help you tap into the power available to you?

_____
_____
_____
_____
_____
_____

How can you testify of God's forgiveness and restoration? Do you ever struggle with accepting His acceptance of you?

_____
_____
_____
_____
_____
_____

Samson was restored to his faith at the last, but he died tragically and prematurely, forfeiting many blessings. If someone you know is ignoring the dangers of sin in their life, how can you reach out to them lovingly with God's truth?

_____
_____
_____
_____
_____
_____

I praise You, Lord, for the good things You are going to do in my life.

...Abraham...became the father of many nations, **according to what was spoken***, "So shall your descendants be." And* **not being weak in faith, he did not...waver** *at the* **promise of God** *through* **unbelief***, but was* **strengthened in faith, giving glory to God***.*

Romans 4:16-20

Why did Abraham have strong faith? Because God spoke to him and gave him a promise. Without a word from God, there can be no faith. You cannot ask God for faith about anything if you're merely guessing at His will. You must first have a promise from God.

Faith is not man's way of getting man's will done in heaven; it is God's way of getting God's will done on earth. God has not promised, "If you have enough faith, I'll do whatever you want." But many people believe this way. If that were the case, you'd be in control instead of God. *What good is a God you can control?* It is God Who dispenses faith (Rom. 12:3), and He's not going to give you faith for anything that is outside of His will. That's why the whole "name it and claim it" concept is absurd. You cannot name it until God claims it. You've got to hear from God in order to have faith.

Faith is a response to the Word of God. God spoke, and Abraham without hesitation said, "Yes, Sir. That's right, Lord." In believing the promise, Abraham was believing the Promiser. God honored his faith and strengthened it even further. Abraham's next response bolstered his faith all the more! He gave glory to God for the miraculous things He was going to be doing in and through him. There's a reciprocal action that takes place when praise and faith intertwine. Praise strengthens faith and faith strengthens praise. Praise makes faith shout. And when faith hears the shout of praise, it grows stronger and stronger.

When God speaks to you, when He gives you a promise, praise Him for it. Glorify Him for what He's going to do as He fulfills His will and accomplishes His purposes in your life. As you praise Him, you'll find faith growing steadily stronger in your heart.

Do you respond to God without hesitation or reservation, as Abraham did? What insights did you find today about ways to strengthen your faith?

_____
_____
_____
_____
_____
_____

How often do you praise God for what He *will be doing* in your life, as His future plans for you unfold? What effects could this have on your faith?

_____
_____
_____
_____
_____
_____

If someone you know adheres to the misconception about having enough faith to get whatever they want from God—how could you show them the truth about seeking God's will and His promises?

_____
_____
_____
_____
_____
_____

Lord, give me faith strong enough to include an "if not" clause.

Shadrach, Meshach, and Abed-Nego answered..."O Nebuchadnezzar, we have **no need to answer you** in this matter. If that is the case, **our God** whom we serve **is able to deliver us** from the burning fiery furnace, **and He will deliver us** from your hand, O king. **But if not**, let it be known...that **we do not serve your gods**, nor will we worship the gold image which you have set up."

DANIEL 3:16-18

Confronted by the king and presented with a choice, Shadrach, Meshach, and Abednego didn't even need a moment to confer. There was no question as to what they were going to do; so no answer need be given. These young men were not going to compromise their faith. They weren't going to have anything to do with idols or foreign gods. Irate king and fiery furnace or not, the matter was already settled in their hearts. So there was nothing to decide.

There was also no question about God's ability to save them from a fiery death, if it was His will to do so. They knew God *could* deliver them from the fire, or even *in* the fire; they knew He **would** deliver them from the evil king who was demanding they act contrary to God's commands. Even if they died in the furnace, they would be free from his tyrannical grip.

The only question was: how would God's sovereign plan for them unfold? These young men didn't know what the outcome would be as they were there facing certain death. Yet they stood firm and said, "We refuse to disgrace our God and dishonor our faith. We're going to stand up for what's right, whether we're delivered or not. We're not going to bow to your idol."

It's one thing to have faith for deliverance; it's another thing to have faith to face death and remain steadfast in your convictions. You'd better have an "if not" clause in your faith. It may not be long before you find yourself in some incendiary circumstance. Your faith may be in the fire and you'll need to stand firm, trusting God to honor the faith that honors Him.

TAPESTRY

Does your faith have an 'if not' clause? God is able to deliver you from trials and troubles, but if He doesn't, will you still trust Him? Obey Him? Serve Him?

_____
_____
_____
_____
_____
_____

For kids coming up in a world of "tolerance" and compromise, how could you help instill in their hearts and lives this kind of steadfast faith to help them stand firm when challenged?

_____
_____
_____
_____
_____
_____

You might take a moment to read back over the full story (Dan. 3) as you think of how "fire-proof" faith could powerfully impact others.

_____
_____
_____
_____
_____
_____

Thank You, Lord that I never have to face a trial or heartache alone.

*...Others were tortured, **not accepting deliverance**, that they might obtain a **better** resurrection. **Still others**...were stoned, they were sawn in two... afflicted, tormented...And **all these**, having obtained **a good testimony through faith**, did not **receive the promise**, God having provided **something better for us**...*

HEBREWS 11:35-40

Reading Hebrews 11, we're inspired by all the marvelous testimonies of what God can do through people of faith. Exciting stories of victory and deliverance make us want to emulate those saints who had such triumphs of faith...until we come to these *others*...who would seem more like *failures* of faith.

But these "others" loved God and trusted in Him just as much as those who were delivered out of trouble. Their testimony of faith is just as strong. Some escaped by faith, while some endured by faith.

God has not promised that we would not know difficulty. In fact, He has promised that *in* trials we'll know ultimate victory:

> Who shall separate us from the love of Christ? Shall tribulation, or distress, or persecution...or peril, or sword? As it is written: "For Your sake we are killed all day long"...Yet in all these things we are more than conquerors through Him who loved us" (Rom. 8:35-37).

Yes, even the victorious walk through deepest trials. God has not promised that we won't have trials or even that we'll escape unscathed. But He has promised never to leave or forsake us. (Heb. 13:5) Faith is not so much receiving from God what we want as it is accepting from God what He gives or what He allows.

God has also promised that His ultimate purpose will be fulfilled. Those who endured by faith trusted the steadfast promises of God and looked to a better future. God's wonderful plans for eternity include all who have lived and died by faith. It may be any day when He returns to fulfill His promises to them and to us! That's why we, too, should be living with a hopeful eye to the future and a faith that is resting on the eternal promises of God.

Think of God's steadfast promises for the future and the wonderful plans He has for our eternity with Him and all those who have lived and died by faith. What words of thanksgiving and praise come to your mind?

_____
_____
_____
_____
_____
_____

Do you have enough faith to be in the "others" crowd? If God doesn't deliver you from suffering, how will you resolve to trust His promises—and keep serving Him?

_____
_____
_____
_____
_____
_____

If someone you know has been enduring difficulties or heartaches for some time, consider how you could use these truths to encourage them today.

_____
_____
_____
_____
_____
_____

Thank You, Lord, for Your limitless grace and abundant mercy.

*Then one of the criminals...blasphemed Him, saying, "If You are the Christ, save Yourself and us." But the other...rebuked him, saying, "Do you not even **fear God**, seeing you are under the same **condemnation**? And we indeed **justly**...but **this Man has done nothing** wrong." Then he said to Jesus, "**Lord, remember me when** You come into **Your kingdom**." And Jesus said to him, "**Assuredly**...today you will be with Me in Paradise."*

Luke 23:39-43

Three men were dying at Calvary. As Jesus, the God-man, was dying for the sins of the world, two thieves hung beside Him, receiving their due punishment. One died in his sin, refusing Christ. But the other called on Jesus, died *to* his sin, and is now in heaven. His brief prayer doesn't seem like much, but it counted for eternity.

Perhaps he saw how Jesus treated those who mistreated Him or heard Him pray, "Father, forgive them..." (v. 34). Whatever caused this man to utter that prayer, he clearly had a grasp on some truths. He knew some things you'll have to know to be absolutely certain you're going to heaven.

He knew he was a sinner who was getting what he deserved (Rom. 6:23), and he had a healthy fear of a holy God. Somehow this man knew that Jesus was completely sinless. He also saw Him as sovereign. He called Jesus *Lord*, using a term which means "very God of very God." He knew Jesus was going to reign, speaking of "when", not *if*, He would enter His kingdom. He had no doubt this One Who had been mocked, beaten, rejected—and *crucified* would one day rule. Talk about faith!

This condemned man saw Jesus as Savior. He knew there was nothing he could do except what Romans 10:13 says to do: "For 'whoever calls on the name of the Lord shall be saved.'" *Whoever* means anybody, any place, any time—even a dying thief who prays, "Lord, remember me." When you're saved by God's grace, you are saved instantly and forever. How did this man *know* he was going to heaven? Jesus told him: "**Assuredly**."

Tapestry

Think of God's promises to you. Are you living in assurance of those things? Where do you need to exhibit more faith?

_____
_____
_____
_____
_____
_____

One man put his utmost trust in Jesus while one chose to jeer with the crowd that day. What things might soften a person's heart toward Christ, and what could cause someone to be so hardened they're unable to reach out in faith?

_____
_____
_____
_____
_____
_____

With his dying breath, this criminal called out to Jesus and was saved. How can you use his story to encourage others to hold out hope and keep praying for friends and loved ones who need Christ?

_____
_____
_____
_____
_____
_____

Come to Jesus

For all have sinned and fall short of the glory of God.

—Romans 3:23

..."Believe on the Lord Jesus Christ, and you will be saved..."

—Acts 16:31

If we confess our sins, He is faithful and just to forgive us our sins and to cleanse us from all unrighteousness.

—1 John 1:9

...if any man be in Christ, he is a new creature: old things are passed away; behold, all things are become new.

—2 Corinthians 5:17

"Therefore whoever confesses Me before men, him I will also confess before My Father Who is in heaven."

—Matthew 10:32

*Then he said to Jesus, "**Lord, remember me** when You come into Your kingdom." And Jesus said to him, "Assuredly, I say to you, **today you will be with Me in Paradise."***

—Luke 23:42-43

This thief who was crucified next to Jesus was given more in a moment than he had stolen in a lifetime. He went straight to Heaven from that cross. (2 Cor. 5:8) Jesus wants you to join Him in Paradise, too! All it takes is a simple, sincere act of faith, just as this man demonstrated. Like him, you must see yourself as a sinner and understand that there is a holy God Whose wrath burns against sin. You must recognize Jesus as the sinless, sovereign, saving Christ Who died in your place. Then willingly turn from your sin to Jesus and pray, "Lord, remember me."

Right now, you can put your faith where God has placed your sins—on Jesus. You might pray something like this:

> *Dear God, I'm a sinner and my sin deserves judgment. I know You love me and You want to save me. Jesus, You paid my sin debt with Your blood on the cross. You died and rose again that I might have life. I lift my hand of faith now to receive Your gift of grace. Come into my heart, forgive my sin and save me. You're now my Lord, my Savior, my God and my friend. I stand on Your Word and receive it by faith, and that settles it. Give me the courage to step out in obedience, Lord, and show my faith publicly so You can begin to make me the person You want me to be. In Your Name I pray, Amen.*

And if you have done that just now, take the next step by finding a Bible-believing church where you can openly confess your faith in Christ through believer's baptism. Pray about joining with a local body of believers who can welcome you into their fellowship and help you to grow in your newfound faith. Stay in God's Word, continuing to hear from Him each day, and learn to live a victorious life of faith and forgiveness as you rely on Christ living in and through you every step of the way!

The greatest miracle is the salvation of a soul. **No other miracle cost God anything.** When God made this world, He simply spoke and it was so. **When He healed** a blind man, caused a lame person to walk or cast demons from someone...**all He had to do was say so**, and they were **healed. But to save a soul, God had to hang His dear Son on a cross.** The only time **God** went to any **difficulty** to do anything was **Calvary**. The greatest miracle is the **healing of a sin-sick soul.**

—Adrian Rogers

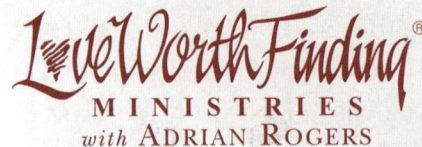

For helpful resources go to: www.lwf.org
You can also contact Love Worth Finding Ministries at: 1-800-274-5683

Dr. Adrian P. Rogers
September 12, 1931 – November 15, 2005

Dr. Adrian Rogers, one of America's most respected Bible teachers, faithfully preached the Word of God for 54 years—32 of those as senior pastor of Bellevue Baptist Church near Memphis, Tennessee. He was gifted with a unique ability to communicate God's Word with clarity and compassion. He wrote 18 books and over 50 booklets helping people apply biblical principles to many subjects and areas of life—including prophecy, marriage, evangelism and the Christian walk.

In 1987 he founded Love Worth Finding Ministries to share the glorious Gospel of Jesus Christ with millions around the world. Today, that multimedia ministry proclaims the Good News globally each day through radio, television and the Internet. The ministry also provides unique publications like this journal to help people deepen their love for the Lord and for His Word.

His faith became sight in November 2005, and doubtless he has experienced the joy of laying many crowns at the feet of his precious Savior. We continue to be grateful for the gifts God bestowed upon Adrian Rogers and for how he humbly gave those back to the Lord—and is therefore still being used of God in a mighty way! His heartbeat was to bring people to Jesus and to help them know and love Him more and more each day. That powerful work continues because of the rare anointing of God upon Dr. Rogers' ministry, and we pray that many more souls will **come to Jesus** as a result of his legacy.

All of Pastor Adrian Rogers' messages were characterized by his unique wit and wisdom which so often brought truths to life in memorable ways. So we'd like to close out this journal with a small collection of his quotes—some amusing, some insightful—taken from the various sermons used to create Tapestry: Faith & Forgiveness. May they leave you with a smile on your face, some joy in your heart and an even deeper desire to explore the riches of God's grace which are ours through faith!

There's hardly a boy or girl who doesn't know the story of Daniel in the lion's den—how God gave those lions lockjaw and Daniel trusted the Lord, pulled up a lion, made a fluffy pillow out of him, got out his Old Testament and began to read between the lions—just having a wonderful time, doing his devotions. We love that. (You don't love the pun, but you love the story. The pun is part of your *punishment*...)

One lady was asked, "What do you believe?" She said, "Well, I believe what my church believes." "What does your church believe?" "Well, my church believes what I believe." "Well, what do you both believe?" "Well, we both believe the same thing."

I heard about a little boy who got saved at children's church. And the children's minister said to him, "Now go over there and tell the pastor you've been saved and you want to get baptized." But the little fellow had not been in church much and he didn't know a lot of terminology. So he went over and told the pastor this: "I've been saved and I need to get **advertised**."—Amen?

You may be wondering, "If God can do all of those things—if He can raise the dead, heal the lame—why doesn't God do something?" **It's like the little boy who said, "If God's so great, why didn't He put the vitamins in ice cream rather than spinach?"** Why doesn't God do it the way I want Him to do it?

Now there are those so-called theologians who want to re-examine the Bible today. **I'd just as soon trust a group of blind men with some lightning bugs in a jar in a dark cave trying to examine the noonday sun than these people to examine the Word of God.** As far as I'm concerned, we need to re-examine these so-called theologians.

If you want God to explain everything to you, forget it. Number one, you couldn't understand it; number two, God's not going to limit Himself to what you could understand. I had oatmeal for breakfast this morning, and Joyce put some milk on it for me. I couldn't have that if I'd needed understanding. **How can a brown cow eat green grass and give white milk that churns yellow butter?** I don't understand that. You don't understand that. Folks, even the simplest things we don't understand. We don't live by explanations.

I read about a man whose office files were getting so full of extraneous papers. He was a man who couldn't bear to throw anything away, and the files got fuller and fuller and fuller. One day, his secretary said, "Sir, can I clean out the files?" He said, "Well, okay, clean them out. But before you throw anything away, make a copy of it." Is that the way we forgive? You know, "I'm going to get rid of it, but I'm going to remember it." No, you forget it. Forgive finally.

notes

NOTES

NOTES

NOTES

Notes

NOTES

NOTES

NOTES

NOTES

notes